THIS MOMENT

BOLD VOICES FROM WRITEGIRL

WriteGirl Publications • Los Angeles

ALSO FROM WRITEGIRL PUBLICATIONS

Sound Generation: *The Resonant Voices of Teen Girls*
Emotional Map of Los Angeles: *Creative Voices from WriteGirl*
You Are Here: *The WriteGirl Journey*
No Character Limit: *Truth & Fiction from WriteGirl*
Intensity: *The 10th Anniversary Anthology from WriteGirl*
Beyond Words: *The Creative Voices of WriteGirl*
Silhouette: *Bold Lines & Voices from WriteGirl*
Listen to Me: *Shared Secrets from WriteGirl*
Lines of Velocity: *Words That Move from WriteGirl*
Untangled: *Stories & Poetry from the Women and Girls of WriteGirl*
Nothing Held Back: *Truth & Fiction from WriteGirl*
Pieces of Me: *The Voices of WriteGirl*
Bold Ink: *Collected Voices of Women and Girls*
Threads
Pens on Fire: *Creative Writing Experiments for Teens from WriteGirl (Curriculum Guide)*

IN-SCHOOLS PROGRAM ANTHOLOGIES

Unstoppable: *Creative Voices of the WriteGirl & Bold Ink Writers In-Schools Programs*
These Moments: *The Creative Voices of the WriteGirl In-Schools Program*
Words & Curiosity: *Creative Voices of the WriteGirl In-Schools Program*
This Is My World: *Creative Voices of the WriteGirl In-Schools Program*
Ready for the Next Chapter: *Creative Voices of the WriteGirl In-Schools Program*
No Matter What: *Creative Voices from the WriteGirl In-Schools Program*
So Much to Say: *The Creative Voices of the WriteGirl In-Schools Program*
Sound of My Voice: *Bold Words from the WriteGirl In-Schools Program*
This Is Our Space: *Bold Words from the WriteGirl In-Schools Program*
Ocean of Words: *Bold Voices from the WriteGirl In-Schools Program*
Reflections: *Creative Writing from Destiny Girls Academy*
Afternoon Shine: *Creative Writing from the Bold Ink Writers Program at the Marc & Eva Stern Math and Science School*
Words That Echo: *Creative Writing from Downey, Lawndale and Lynwood Cal-SAFE Schools*
The Landscape Ahead: *Creative Writing from New Village Charter High Schools*
Sometimes, Just Sometimes: *Creative Writing from La Vida West and Lynwood Cal-SAFE Programs*
Everything About Her: *Creative Writing from New Village High School*
Visible Voices: *Creative Writing from Destiny Girls Academy*
Now That I Think About It: *Creative Writing from Destiny Girls Academy*
Look at Me Long Enough: *Creative Writing from Destiny Girls Academy*

Acclaim for WriteGirl Publications

"The written words of these young women represent small acts of courage. They are not only proclaiming they have something to say but owning their voices, and thereby reminding us all that they matter."

– Erica Shelton Kodish, television writer of *The Good Wife, Being Mary Jane* and *Cold Case*

"Every WriteGirl anthology is as unique as the voices and lives of the young women and girls whose writings fill these pages. For anyone taking the brave leap of sharing a view through the windows of what it's like to be a person in the world, with both the love and pain of it all, gives a blessing to both the writers and readers."

– Louise Goffin, singer-songwriter, GRAMMY®-nominated producer and co-host of *The Great Song Adventure* podcast

"There has never been a more important moment to amplify the voices of young women and allow them an arena to speak their truth, own their story and express their creativity."

– Rory Green, author, workshop leader and creator of Write to Be You Reflective Writing Circles

"[*This Moment*] is an absolute must-read that bursts at the seams with unique and talented voices showing us what it means to be a young woman today. Passion shimmers on every page, with a very real sense of craft woven throughout. The collective words of all these young women will change you ... for the better."

– Marissa Kennerson, YA author of *Tarot* and *The Family*

"Stepping out from the shadows are voices that must be heard, starting with these girls who are taking over the world."

– Lisa Freeman, YA author of the *Honey Girl* series

"The symphony of the teenaged experience is precisely why WriteGirl exists — to capture the sloppiness and the art of being alive."

– Heather Hach Hearne, screenwriter of *Freaky Friday* and *What to Expect When You're Expecting* and librettist for *Legally Blonde — The Musical*

"The only thing more inspiring than WriteGirl, the organization, is the girls themselves. Their process is a combination of work and play, craft and self-exploration. The results are kind of mind-boggling!"

– Josann McGibbon, screenwriter of *Descendants, Runaway Bride* and *The Starter Wife*

"The name could just as easily be 'Write, Girl!' — an exhortation for a young woman to take her life, her future, her sense of self into her own hands by putting a pen there. Nothing has the sheer human power to change minds and hearts than a simply and beautifully wrought sentence has. Write, girls!"

– Patt Morrison, *Los Angeles Times* columnist, radio host for KPCC and best-selling author

"Adolescents reading this anthology will recognize themselves in the words. Aspiring wordsmiths can use the works as models for their own writing or try their turn at the various exercises in the book."

– *School Library Journal*

"What these girls have to say makes us laugh at times, and other times makes us want to cry. But their words always make us believe. These girls understand the power of words."

– Meg Cabot, author of *The Princess Diaries, Allie Finkle's Rules for Girls* and *Size 12 and Ready to Rock*

"I have never owned a WriteGirl anthology that didn't eventually make the rounds of my friends. The writing is fine writing, and that the authors are young writers makes no difference. Art is art. Good writing is good writing. And every emotion finds genuine expression."

– Eloise Klein Healy, past Poet Laureate of Los Angeles

"These girls started with a few words and the seed of an idea. With WriteGirl's encouragement, each girl allowed the words to keep coming until her idea grew into an essay, a story or a poem. What do writers do? They write. And how lucky we are to have these writers' words and ideas to inspire us!"

– Carole King, GRAMMY® Award-winning singer and songwriter

"Powerful and strong, raw and vulnerable — these are the voices of girls who demand to be heard. ... You will not only hear them, but you'll never forget them."

– Kami Garcia, *New York Times* best-selling author of *Beautiful Creatures*

"Having a group like WriteGirl is an amazing help to those who love the craft. The mentoring of the young girls is a wonderful way to pair the professional with the new writers to show them how to hone their skills and have a successful career doing so."

– Diane Warren, GRAMMY® Award-winning songwriter of "Because You Loved Me"

"Cheers to Keren Taylor for coming up with the dream of giving teenage girls a voice, and then creating an organization that made her dream a reality. Cheers also for her hardworking staff, and the dedicated volunteers and mentors of WriteGirl for enabling teenage girls to wrestle the truth of their lives, their hearts and souls, into literary form on the page."

– Barbara Abercrombie, UCLA Extension creative writing instructor and author of *Kicking in the Wall: A Year of Writing Exercises, Prompts, and Quotes to Help You Break Through Your Blocks and Reach Your Writing Goals*

"I love hearing the new voices in these pages. I've had the pleasure of being part of one of WriteGirl's workshops. Now when I meet a young woman in her teens who asks for advice on becoming a writer, I instantly say, 'Have you heard of WriteGirl? Get involved with them immediately!'"

– Robin Swicord, screenwriter of *The Curious Case of Benjamin Button* and *Memoirs of a Geisha*, and screenwriter-director of *The Jane Austen Book Club*

"Sharp observations abound ... unconventional writing exercises ... motivational quotes ... nonstop inspiration."

– *Publishers Weekly*

"All I ever think about is how to make more young women want to share their voices with the world — and WriteGirl, plus this anthology, are actually doing it. There's nothing cooler than jumping into the worlds of these young women as well as the minds of the brilliant women who mentor them."

– Jill Soloway, writer-producer of *Transparent* and author of *Tiny Ladies in Shiny Pants*

AWARDS FOR WRITEGIRL PUBLICATIONS

2018 **Winner**, Next Generation Indie Book Awards, Anthology: *Sound Generation: The Resonant Voices of Teen Girls*

2018 **Winner**, International Book Awards, Anthology: *Sound Generation: The Resonant Voices of Teen Girls*

2018 **Winner**, National Indie Excellence Awards, Anthology: *Sound Generation: The Resonant Voices of Teen Girls*

2018 **Winner**, Los Angeles Book Festival, Anthology: *Sound Generation: The Resonant Voices of Teen Girls*

2018 **Winner**, Great Southwest Book Festival, Compilations: *Sound Generation: The Resonant Voices of Teen Girls*

2017 **Winner**, Southern California Book Festival, Anthology: *Sound Generation: The Resonant Voices of Teen Girls*

2017 **Runner-Up**, London Book Festival, Anthology: *Sound Generation: The Resonant Voices of Teen Girls*

2017 **Winner**, Pinnacle Book Achievement Award, Young Adult: *Sound Generation: The Resonant Voices of Teen Girls*

2017 **Winner**, Beverly Hills Book Awards, Anthology: *Sound Generation: The Resonant Voices of Teen Girls*

2017 **Award Finalist**, Best Book Awards, Anthology: *Sound Generation: The Resonant Voices of Teen Girls*

2015 **Winner**, International Book Awards, Anthology: *Emotional Map of Los Angeles*

2015 **Winner**, National Indie Excellence Awards, Anthology: *Emotional Map of Los Angeles*

2015 **Finalist**, Next Generation Indie Book Awards, Anthology: *Emotional Map of Los Angeles*

2015 **Winner**, Beverly Hills Book Awards, Anthology: *Emotional Map of Los Angeles*

2015 **Runner-Up**, Great Southwest Book Festival, Young Adult: *Emotional Map of Los Angeles*

2015 **Honorable Mention**, Los Angeles Book Festival, Young Adult: *Emotional Map of Los Angeles*

2015 **Finalist**, ForeWord Reviews' INDIEFAB Book of the Year Award, Anthologies: *Emotional Map of Los Angeles*

2015 **Finalist**, USA Best Book Awards, Young Adult: Nonfiction: *Emotional Map of Los Angeles*

2015 **Runner-Up**, Southern California Book Festival, Compilations/Anthologies: *Emotional Map of Los Angeles*

2015 **Winner**, Pinnacle Book Achievement Award, Young Adult: *Emotional Map of Los Angeles*

2014 **Honorable Mention**, Hollywood Book Festival: *You Are Here*

2014 **Finalist**, USA Best Book Awards, Compilations/Anthologies: *You Are Here*

2014 **Winner**, The Great Midwest Book Festival, Compilations/Anthologies: *You Are Here*

2014 **Winner**, International Book Awards, Young Adult: *You Are Here*

2014 **Winner**, Beverly Hills Book Awards, Anthologies: *You Are Here*

2014 **Runner-Up**, Great Northwest Book Festival: *You Are Here*

2014 **Runner-Up**, Great Southwest Book Festival: *You Are Here*

2014 **Finalist, Silver Medal**, Next Generation Indie Book Awards: *You Are Here*

2014 **Honorable Mention**, San Francisco Book Festival: *You Are Here*

2014 **Honorable Mention**, Paris Book Festival: *You Are Here*

2014 **Honorable Mention**, New York Book Festival: *You Are Here*

2014 **Honorable Mention**, Los Angeles Book Festival: *You Are Here*

2014 **Honorable Mention**, London Book Festival: *You Are Here*

2013 **Silver Medal**, Independent Publisher Book Awards: *No Character Limit*

2013 **Winner**, IndieReader Discovery Awards, Anthologies: *No Character Limit*

2013 **Honorable Mention**, Eric Hoffer Award, Young Adult: *No Character Limit*

2013 **Bronze**, ForeWord Reviews Book of the Year Awards, Anthologies: *No Character Limit*

2013 **Finalist**, International Book Awards, Anthologies: *No Character Limit*

2013 **Finalist**, Next Generation Indie Book Awards, Anthologies: *No Character Limit*

2013 **Honorable Mention**, San Francisco Book Festival, Anthologies: *No Character Limit*

2013 **Honorable Mention**, Paris Book Festival, Anthologies: *No Character Limit*

2013 **Runner-Up**, Great Southwest Book Festival, Anthologies: *No Character Limit*

2012 **Finalist**, Beverly Hills Book Awards, Anthologies: *No Character Limit*

2012 **Winner**, USA Best Book Awards, Anthologies: *No Character Limit*

2012 **Runner-Up**, London Book Festival, Anthologies: *No Character Limit*

2012 **Winner**, Los Angeles Book Festival, Anthologies: *No Character Limit*

2012 **Runner-Up**, Southern California Book Festival, Anthologies: *No Character Limit*

2012 **Honorable Mention**, Eric Hoffer Award, Young Adult: *Intensity*

2012 **Winner**, International Book Awards, Anthologies: Nonfiction: *Intensity*

2012 **Winner**, National Indie Excellence Awards, Anthologies: *Intensity*

2012 **Runner-Up**, San Francisco Book Festival Awards, Anthologies: *Intensity*

2012 **Runner-Up**, Paris Book Festival Awards, Anthologies: *Intensity*

2011 **Finalist**, ForeWord Reviews Book of the Year Awards, Anthologies: *Intensity*

2011 **Honorable Mention**, Los Angeles Book Festival, Anthologies: *Intensity*

2011 **Winner**, London Book Festival Awards, Anthologies: *Intensity*

2011 **Honorable Mention**, New England Book Festival, Anthologies: *Intensity*

2011 **Finalist**, USA Best Book Awards, Anthologies, Nonfiction: *Intensity*

2011 **Winner**, International Book Awards, Anthologies, Nonfiction: *Beyond Words*

2011 **Winner**, National Indie Excellence Awards, Anthologies: *Beyond Words*

2011 **Finalist**, Next Generation Indie Book Awards, Anthologies: *Beyond Words*

2011 **Finalist**, Independent Book Publisher Awards, Anthologies: *Beyond Words*

2010 **Finalist**, ForeWord Reviews Book of the Year Awards, Anthologies: *Beyond Words*

2010 **Winner**, London Book Festival, Anthologies: *Beyond Words*

2010 **Winner**, National Best Book Awards, USA Book News, Poetry: *Beyond Words*

2010 **First Place**, National Indie Excellence Awards, Anthologies: *Silhouette*

2010 **Winner**, New York Book Festival, Teenage: *Silhouette*

2010 **Winner**, International Book Awards, Anthologies: *Silhouette*

2009 **Winner**, London Book Festival Awards, Anthologies: *Silhouette*

2009 **Finalist**, ForeWord Reviews Book of the Year Awards: *Silhouette*

2009 **Winner**, Los Angeles Book Festival, Nonfiction: *Silhouette*

2009 **Winner**, National Best Book Awards, USA Book News, Anthologies: *Silhouette*

2009 **Silver Medal**, Independent Publisher Book Awards: *Listen to Me*

2009 **Runner-Up**, San Francisco Book Festival, Teenage: *Listen to Me*

2009 **Winner**, National Indie Excellence Awards, Anthologies: *Listen to Me*

2009 **Runner-Up**, New York Book Festival, Teenage: *Listen to Me*

2009 **Finalist**, Next Generation Indie Book Awards: *Listen to Me*

2008 **Finalist**, ForeWord Reviews: *Listen to Me*

2008 **Winner**, London Book Festival Awards, Teenage: *Lines of Velocity*

2008 **Honorable Mention**, New England Books Festival, Anthologies: *Lines of Velocity*

2008 **Grand Prize Winner**, Next Generation Indie Book Awards: *Lines of Velocity*

2008 **Winner**, National Best Book Awards, USA Book News: *Lines of Velocity*

2008 **Silver Medal**, Independent Publisher Awards: *Lines of Velocity*

2008 **Honorable Mention**, New York Festival of Books Awards: *Lines of Velocity*

2007 **Finalist**, ForeWord Magazine: *Lines of Velocity*

2007 **Honorable Mention**, London Book Festival Awards: *Untangled*

2006 **Finalist**, ForeWord Magazine: *Untangled*

2006 **Winner**, National Best Book Awards, USA Book News: *Untangled*

2006 **Notable Mention**, Writers Notes Magazine Book Awards: *Nothing Held Back*

2006 **Honorable Mention**, Independent Publisher Book Awards: *Nothing Held Back*

2005 **Finalist**, Independent Publisher Awards: *Pieces of Me*

2005 **Finalist**, ForeWord Magazine: *Bold Ink*

WriteGirl Publications . Los Angeles

This Moment: Bold Voices from WriteGirl

Executive Editor: Keren Taylor

Associate Editors: Allison Deegan
Katie Geyer
Kirsten Giles

Book Manager: Annlee Ellingson

Assistant Editors: Julia Black
Amanda Mercedes
Corinna McClanahan Schroeder

Production Manager: Beka Badila

Production Support: Heather Alexander
Megan Bennett
Christina Brown
Olivia Butze
Cindy Collins
Cat Manabat
Lindsay Miller
Kelsey O'Brien
Bonita Thompson

Art Director: Keren Taylor
Book Design: Juliana Sankaran-Felix
Cover Design: Sara Apelkvist
Printing: Chromatic Inc., Los Angeles

Library of Congress Cataloging-in-Publication Data

Names: Taylor, Keren - author
Title: This Moment: Bold Voices from WriteGirl / Keren Taylor
Description: First Edition. | Los Angeles, CA : WriteGirl Publications, [2019]
Identifiers: LCCN 2019942549 | ISBN 978-0-578-49912-3
LC record available at https://lccn.loc.gov/2019942549

FIRST EDITION
Printed in the United States of America
Orders, inquiries and correspondence:
WriteGirl Publications
Los Angeles, California
www.writegirl.org | info@writegirl.org | 213-253-2655

Acknowledgements

All of us at WriteGirl wish to extend our heartfelt thanks to each and every one of you who helped make this anthology possible.

Two years have passed since the publication of our last anthology, and it is with great pride and excitement that we bring you *This Moment: Bold Voices from WriteGirl*. The book team dove into a sea of submissions from our teens (and a few of our alums) that included poetry, prose, songs, and excerpts from novels and screenplays. It has been both a labor of love and an honor to read through the hundreds of pages of submissions sent to us via email, snail mail, text, hand delivery and even snapshots of handwritten pieces. Some pieces were quickly scribbled down at one of our monthly workshops while others were labored over during weekly mentor-mentee writing sessions.

Thank you to all our WriteGirl volunteers for your passion and dedication. You provide the safe and inspiring space in which our girls can explore their voices and share their words freely both on the page and out loud. Your enormous contribution of time and expertise is the foundation for the growth of WriteGirl, and the impact of your efforts will ripple out into the community for many decades to come.

We would like to thank our WriteGirl parents. We are grateful for your support in encouraging your daughters to participate in our workshops and mentoring sessions, and driving them to special events all over Los Angeles County.

To our board members, friends and supporters, thank you for helping sustain WriteGirl year after year. You make it possible for us to expand and enhance our programming and our reach. To all our partners in the community and our in-kind donors, we thank you for your outstanding generosity.

Thank you to our book manager Annlee Ellingson and the entire book team of editors, proofreaders and production assistants. Your long hours, late nights, intensive focus and patience made this book possible.

Thank you to Sara Apelkvist for designing the cover of this book and for your infinite care for all the details, and to Juliana Sankaran-Felix for showcasing the writing in a way that honors and celebrates our girls' words and the spirit of WriteGirl.

Finally, a big thank you to every WriteGirl teen writer. Your creativity and profound courage bring this anthology to life!

This Moment: **Table of Contents**

Foreword by Lauren Graham 20

Introduction by Keren Taylor 22

1. My Essence: **Identity**

Acquired Taste ◆ Madison Huggins 25
Tamarind ◆ Aleea Evangelista 26
Three Lives ◆ Sophie Rosenblum 27
Caught between Two Worlds ◆ Alejandra Rodriguez 28
Different Body, Same Mind ◆ Zoe Frohna 30
No Real Name ◆ Kiyanti Schlank 32
Stuck in the Middle ◆ Sophia Rutt 34
I Wish I Could Tell Her ◆ Nicole Jefferson 36
Hide and Seek ◆ Helen Graham 37
Ni de aquí, ni de allá ◆ Lauren Thielen 38
My Bubble ◆ Kayla Veloz 39
no Name ◆ Emmett Thompson 40

2. Never More Than a Text Apart: **Friendship**

Space Bends for Us, Miles Mean Nothing ◆ Culzean Giammatteo 43
The Four Amigas ◆ Natalie Mendez 44
"What Are You Doing?" ◆ Samantha Becaria 45
Eren's Caramel Angel ◆ Emily Tuckness-Kuntz 46
Drive ◆ Annie Son 47
Rushing It ◆ Sarah Carter 48
Will You Jump With Me? ◆ Brandy Mendoza 50
What I Regret Saying ◆ Alyssa Ho 51
Queen ◆ Taya Kendall 52

3. We Step Forward: **Growing Up**

All Those Times ◆ Kate Lewis 55
Unrecognizable Memories ◆ Savannah House 56
The Ringer ◆ Pearl Dickson 57
(The Things I Left Behind in) New York City ◆ Sophia Moore 58
Parties ◆ Zoe Frohna 59
The Quiet Life ◆ Cora Ries 60
Don't Give Up on Me ◆ Ritika Kandarkar 62
Eulogy to My Teddy Bears ◆ Jazzmin Joya 66

A World, a Sphere ◆ Faiza Meah 67
My Pace ◆ Rhema Vincent 68
Graduation ◆ Culzean Giammatteo 69

4. Read It Out Loud: **News & Society**

From Another Daughter ◆ Sophie Rosenblum 71
La Pauvreté ◆ Gianna Garcia 72
The Do's and Don'ts for Wartime Massacres ◆ Chloë Mirijanian 73
A Terrible Template ◆ Maria Guinnip 74
Guilty ◆ Jacqueline Alvarez 76
The Bathtub ◆ Gillian Chamberlin 77
Let's Meet Angel ◆ Sabina Garcia 78
The Earth Is Not Flat ◆ Olivia Calderon 80
No Place Like Home ◆ Alana Washington 81

5. This Village of Blue: **Colors**

The Odyssey ◆ Allyson Roche 83
We Crossed the County Line Last Night ◆ Addissyn House 84
Orange Peels ◆ Liberty Macias 85
Crown of Gold ◆ Eva Brewster 86
Goodbye ◆ Cristal Rincon 88
Stories ◆ Jane Han 89
A Memory to My Mémère ◆ Zoe Jean-Sprecher 90
Good Morning ◆ Devon Bryce 91

6. Seafood Pizza with My Cousins: **Home**

Kastamu ◆ Bibiana Mashamba 93
Homesick ◆ Makena Ababon 94
July Rain ◆ Phoebe Perkins 96
Mexico Querido ◆ Ariana Cortez 97
Kaleidoscope ◆ Marie Sekiguchi 98
I Want to Go Home ◆ Tindi Mashamba 99
Opening Statement ◆ Lucy Eller 100
First Semester ◆ Chloë Vigil 102
A Piece of Me ◆ Marilyn Marroquin 103

7. When the Light Flickers: **Impermanence**

Rising Flames ◆ Mia Swanson 105
Blue Roses ◆ Sequoia Sherriff 106

Changing Seasons ◆ Valerie Chavez 107
The Invisible Girl ◆ Eden Hirsch 110
Tumor ◆ Macy Kwon 112
Iris ◆ Colette Rogers 113
War ◆ Sofía Salazar 114
Tinted Gray ◆ Hana Saadi-Klein 115
The Change ◆ Lily Mead 116

8. Balms & Powders: **Image**

Walk-in Closet ◆ Faith Alm-Clark 119
Newness ◆ Zoe Jeans 120
Makeup ◆ Samantha Krug 121
Growth ◆ Daniella Josephy 122
Unconventional Art ◆ Diana Balbuena 124
Neutral Palette ◆ Brooke Crocker 125
Deity ◆ Zoe Philadelphia-Kossak 126

9. A Bumpy Ride: **Teen Life**

I Hear Coyotes ◆ Nia Johnson 129
Caught in the Middle ◆ Israa Kawsar 130
The Shadow ◆ Cindy Liu 131
Lemon Meringue Pie ◆ Sofia Silvia 132
And the Winner Is ... ◆ Meagan Harmon 133
pavlov/morning ◆ Miriam Schweiger 134
Journey into the Future ◆ Emma Kim 136
Done. Breathe. Repeat. ◆ Isabel Petty 137
The Secrets of True Jewish Camp ◆ Jamie-Lee Meintjes 138

10. I Have All the Power: **CREATIVITY STARTER KIT**

Introduction: Creativity Starter Kit 141
Writing Experiment: Transform the Ordinary into Something Extraordinary 142
Writing Experiment: If These Walls Could Talk 143
Clock Watches ◆ Lesly Mason 144
Writing Experiment: Turn Memories into Memoir 145
Writing Experiment: Memoir Cut-outs 146
Writing Experiment: Your Creativity Counts — The Nonet 148
Distant Light ◆ Drew Shinozaki 149
Writing Experiment: Take a Journey of Discovery on This Page 150
Writing Experiment: Labyrinth Activity 151

Writing Experiment: Double-Trouble Rhyme-Time 152
Tiny Rhyming Poems • WriteGirl teens and mentors 154
Writing Experiment: Mash-ups: Found Poetry and Acrostic Poems 156
The Leaves Are Burning • Zenopia Aghajanian 157
Writing Experiment: Big Stories in Small Spaces 158
In Here It's Beautiful • Israa Kawsar 159
Writing Experiment: Haiku 160
Songs of Freedom • Zoe Frohna • Tiffany Shin • Daniella Josephy 161

11. Capable of Anything: **Girl Power**

Magnificent Woman • Nyah Toomes 163
Banehag • Alejandra Medina 164
Melanin • Amayah Watson 166
Males vs. Females • Cassie Brennan 168
If Women Were Stars • Arielle Davis 172
Patriart • Clare Margaret Donovan 174
Skating in Pink • Kendra Teraoka 178

12. I Sigh Like a Cartoon: **Relationships**

Amor Fati • Marina Orozco 181
Pretty Girl on Fire • Grace Lyde 182
How I Fell in Love with a Work of Art • Anna Arutunian 183
I Miss You • Anya Baranets 184
Week and 1/2 Dates • Melanie Robles 185
What We Could Have Been • Cashmeir Brown 186
Four Words • Samantha Campbell 188
Emotional • Lena Root 190
Love Train • Akilah Cox 191
But I'm a Pisces • Kaeli McLeod 192
What Changed? • Natalie Pineda 194
An Ode to My Little Rose • Heidy Gisselle Miranda 195
Leave Me Behind • Kaitlyn Esperon 196
Love Poem, or Bananahead • Amber Straw 198
Pink Flowers • Xela Brainin 199
The Kind of Love Story I Want • Addissyn House 200

13. Sneaky Little Balloon: **Whimsy**

Sunlight Smiles • Makena Cioni 203
Marylaine • Sky Bradley 204

An Unexpected Pulse ◆ Cira Davis 205
Fruit Salad ◆ Blossom Bogen-Froese 206
The Man and His Bird ◆ Kendall Arjoon 207
Salted Rope ◆ Clara Ceerla 210
Green Star ◆ Sidny Ramirez 212
The Zamboni ◆ Luna Garcia 213
Her Shadow ◆ Alyssa Ho 214
Amara and the Witch ◆ Sylvia Griffin 215
The Land of Me ◆ Lily Larsen 216

14. Use This Power Wisely: **Modern Life**

Instagram ◆ Elissa Fong 219
Galaxy-sized Thoughts ◆ Jessica Harper 220
- ●● - ●-●● ● ◆ Yousra Kawsar 221
Unplugging ◆ Ashley Ware 222
Through Time ◆ Alyssa Ho 223
Social Media ◆ Juliana Pincus 224
Captcha ◆ Charlie Dodge 226

15. Finally Noticing: **Inspired By**

Living Memories ◆ Galylea Salamanca 231
Paper Planes ◆ Denielle Mancera 232
Just Another Layer ◆ Deborah Shonack 233
Villains Aren't Born ◆ Zoe Gerst 234
Dirty Hands ◆ Indigo Mapa 236
Sour ◆ Scarlett Saldana 237
The Nonexistent Divide Between Land and Air ◆ Hyla Etame 238
An Ode to the Love of the Lonely ◆ Allyson Roche 239
Flames ◆ Ashley Roche 240

16. The Words Sync: **Music**

To You ◆ Courtney Hayforth 243
Where I Belong ◆ Miranda Cheung 244
Stargazer Lilies ◆ Lauren Cook 245
Naturally ◆ Joelly Prado 246
Freedom in the Rain of Words ◆ Hanna Maaloul 248
Ignited ◆ Ana Reyes 249
Young Veins, Old Blood ◆ Catherine Shonack 250
Violin ◆ Annie Min 251
Strike a Chord ◆ Charlotte Shao 252

17. Now It Matters: **Voice**

Limbo's Communiqué ◆ Kumari Billings 255
Mr. Jedrek ◆ Allison Armijo 256
Perspective ◆ Autumn Martin 257
I Lost My Voice ◆ Kianna Teachout 258
Draw Me a Picture ◆ Kimari Cage 259
Creative Insanity ◆ Alexia Furbert 260
Structure ◆ Yvette Aguilar 261
Writer's Fever ◆ Sabrina Youn 262
But It Doesn't Matter ◆ Brielle Bruno 263
Inspiring Sounds ◆ Mina Lee 264

18. Root Deeply: **Nature**

Tree ◆ Annabel Reiher 267
Butterfly Dreams ◆ Belen Gonzalez 268
The Farm ◆ Sophia Richardson 269
Getaway ◆ Serena Holland 270
The Ninth Grade Epiphany ◆ Sydnee Blueford 271
The Senses of the Gardens ◆ Lucy Fung 272
forged in the fire ◆ Kisha Mehta 274
Fallow ◆ Dana Agbede 275
Harmony ◆ Juliana Nicole Fong 276
Wanting ◆ Joanna Zeng 277
You Strike Me ◆ Rachel Alarcio 278

19. Movies Projected on Bedsheets: **Family**

Buenos Aires in Me ◆ Mercedes Solaberrieta 281
My Mother's Love Language ◆ Danielle del Castillo 282
Tomorrow Will Be the Day ◆ Shirley Delgadillo 284
The Arubi ◆ Alexandra Pranger 286
Mom ◆ Isabel Sobrepera 288
Hija Mía ◆ Marcela Hernandez 289
Where I'm From ◆ Ava Chamberlin 290
The Mother ◆ Georgia Minnis 291
Red Light ◆ Dava Braman 292
Family Dinner ◆ Cynthia He 294
Always There ◆ Delilah Brumer 298
Deep Brown ◆ Chloë Mirijanian 299

20. Endless Pit of Positivity: Confidence

Thursday Run • Shani Perez 301
My Place • Machaela McLain 302
Beauty • Madeline Purcell 303
Three Seconds • Maya Pincus 304
Inspirational Quotes • Gabriela Guevara 306
Failure • Isabella Sanchez 307
Just for a Moment • Victoria Rosales 308
Soul Spark • Katie Chung 309
Ocean • Ella Jean-Sprecher 310

21. THIS IS WriteGirl

This Is WriteGirl 312
WriteGirl Works 315
WriteGirl Recognition 316
Alumnae Highlights 318
Mentoring 320
Workshops 321
Special Guests 322
WriteGirl in the Community 324
Bold Futures 325
Publications 326
Lights, Camera, WriteGirl! 328
WriteGirl Leadership 332
WriteGirl Board 334
Partnerships 335
WriteGirl Supporters 336
WriteGirl Would Like to Thank 340

Index 342
About the Editors 346
Connect with WriteGirl 348

Share your story!

Your voice.

The world NEEDS that - for us to share and hear each other's stories. Don't be afraid.

Share!

Foreword

Author and actor Lauren Graham is best known for her roles as Lorelai Gilmore on *Gilmore Girls* and Sarah Braverman on *Parenthood*. She is also a producer and a three-time *New York Times* best seller. Lauren is a WriteGirl mentor and hosted our *Lights, Camera, WriteGirl!* benefit. We're grateful to have Lauren as part of our WriteGirl community!

One day in early 2019, I turned off the news. It wasn't that it was particularly bad — although it wasn't particularly good either — but for the moment I'd had enough. I felt restless. I wanted to stop watching things and instead start to do more ... things. But what? Something helpful. Something hopeful. I thought back, as I often do, to what my father would inevitably say whenever I had a question, or a new interest, or was at a crossroads and needed guidance. "The answer to everything you want to know," he'd say, "is in a book." When I was younger, this statement seemed thrilling yet improbable. Really? The answer to everything? Could that be true? Over the years, I had mostly found the answer to be yes. The written word has been a profound presence in my life, a source of comfort and hope and joy, not to mention an essential aspect of my livelihood as both an actor and a writer. I wished there was a way to share this discovery with a younger generation, I wished there existed some magical place that embodied the values my dad had shown me years ago.

And then I found out about WriteGirl.

With kindness and passion and clarity, Keren Taylor and her team conveyed their mission: to help young girls on their creative journey, to encourage their confidence and to foster their unique voices. How? Through prompts and exercises, and by gathering one-on-one or in larger workshops, writing and sharing and cheering each other on.

Thanks to WriteGirl, I got to work with a mentee who dreams of someday becoming a singer/dancer. She shared her songs and stories with me shyly: she worried they weren't finished or polished or good enough. So many teen girls (so many people!) never get past that first stage, don't ever have a chance to overcome the voice that lurks inside that tells us we aren't good enough and shouldn't dare to express ourselves. At a WriteGirl event, that same mentee had a song of hers put to music by a professional singer. WriteGirl doesn't just tell its girls their dreams are worth having — it shows them what it looks like when they come true.

At the Lights, Camera, WriteGirl! benefit this year, mentees had an opportunity to have their scenes and monologues performed by professional actors, and to get feedback from professional writers. But the true stars were the girls themselves, who laughed and clapped and cheered for their fellow writers. Their pieces were complex and imaginative, and just plain enjoyable. WriteGirl creates opportunities that illustrate to its girls, in word and deed, that their ideas matter, that their songs and poems and stories matter, that they matter.

In these pages you'll find an impressive variety of voices, in a collection united by the shared experience of girls who've thrived in a supportive community of mentors and peers. And this is just the beginning of all these girls will do. With the power of all the words they'll read and write in the future, they just might find the answer to everything.

– Lauren Graham

Introduction

In this moment, these are the voices we should be listening to. The creative words of 180 teen girls burst through the pages of this new anthology — they share their ideas, their emotions and their view of things as they see them right now. And they don't hold back! They offer wisdom, humor, warnings and rallying cries, and there is a fresh vitality here that is worthy of a book, in print, in a volume of 350 pages.

I often think about what the WriteGirl magic is. Did we create a space where women and girls support each other unconditionally, or did teen girls inspire an entire community to be built around their enthusiasm, curiosity and openness? I'm certain it is both things, in simultaneous harmony. Sometimes there is a synchronicity at work — an invisible force that brings people and new ideas together, effortlessly. That is WriteGirl.

The energy and vibe of the WriteGirl community is always sparkling, with hundreds of women and girls trading stories and exploring their creativity in spectacular civic settings such as The Huntington, in the velvet seats of a screening room, or in front of a Rauschenberg multimedia art installation. But this moment, when so many things are truly changing and being illuminated in terms of equity for women — this moment feels different, heightened, even momentous.

We need writers, artists and filmmakers now more than ever to help us reflect on the past, make sense of the present and envision what the future might look like for women, and for all of us. And we need new perspectives from unheard voices to help us get there.

In this moment, these young women share their powerful voices on the page, and give us exactly the inspiration we need.

– **Keren Taylor**, Executive Director

surprise
yourself!

1

My Essence

Identity

Madison Huggins age 17

This piece started in a coffee shop across the table from my WriteGirl mentor, who challenged me to interact with writing according to each of my five senses — a daunting but strangely liberating task.

Acquired Taste

Writing looks like a deserted meadow speckled with yellow and pink and white buds amid a sea of faded green that scrapes your hips as you run. It is peaceful but abundant, and, while beautiful, the silence can be deafening.

Writing feels like running my index finger along the yellowed, flaking edges of a weathered book and smells like the dust particles that coat it. Writing is a rich, dark-tasting thing — like black coffee or cacao or honey.

Writing sounds like leaves beneath a mud-crusted boot or the crackling conversation between logs and a flame. My words are my warmth. The sacred space between the tip of a pen and the surface of a page has been my sanctuary since my days of waddling around the house in a worn Care Bear nightgown, folding a scrap of paper too many times and clumsily stapling the edges into a makeshift book.

Despite the furious tapping of my toes that is almost loud enough to drown out the trembling of my fingertips as I type, I've grown to realize that the magnitude of my fear of writing directly reflects my love for it. Weaving words is just what the bones of my fingers were carved to do. Even the idea of my words having a different pitch when read aloud versus ingested internally, or flopping onto the page with a dull thud instead of the violent excitement with which they pulse through my veins, is crippling.

What is simultaneously the most beautiful and horrifying thing about writing is how something is revealed in the restraint and release of my words — and it is only between the inky blue lines of a page that the tangled pieces of my consciousness can unravel and become tangible and, therefore, conquerable.

Aleea Evangelista age 18

I wrote this poem to make sense of my identity.

Tamarind

Tamarind's sharp bite
clashes with the sticky shrug of rice
reverently soaked in a steaming bath with maternal hands.

I can't decide
between my two halves;
smoked,
breaded in tart disappointment.

Half and half—
and, not or.
Without,
my marrow melts.

I am served on a platter
seared into hand-cut slivers,
doled out in morsels of my finest tissue.
I've simplified my flavor
into an appetizer.

My flavor unforgettable
as you try to
erase my essence.

Sophie Rosenblum age 16

I have come to the conclusion that I have absolutely no idea what my life will look like in a decade. This piece is me looking closer at the possibilities.

Three Lives

Sophie One

I am an executive at a beauty company, one with an eye-catching logo that I loved long before I secured my place at the company. Our building has glass sliding doors between conference rooms and colorful walls where we draw out our thoughts. My desk, propped next to a window, allows for the occasional glance over the city between meetings. The meetings are energizing, our conversation endless. We sit at conference tables and explosively bounce ideas off each other like popcorn. My coworkers and I become friends easily — we bond over books, restaurants, makeup. New York is sharper than I expected — but I like it.

Sophie Two

The rain in Portland hits the roof of the school angrily, which is funny because it's always raining. Why would it be mad? I'm far from angry at the rain — my students come into class more excited to be there because it's an escape from the puddles outside. I finally teach how I wish I was taught when I was a student. We talk about current events and bend the curriculum to fit around the news. We have long, heated discussions, and people get to use their voices. As their teacher I feel proud of everything they accomplish, even beyond the classroom.

Sophie Three

Finally, I'm back in my city, Los Angeles. The light is unbeatable, unique in its way to swallow the city whole, twice a day, in its color. I never tire of it. I'm a screenwriter, and my pilot has just been selected for a reading by the next round of executives, something that makes my stomach ache and my feet tap restlessly. I've been working on this for years, and it could be turned down within minutes. Life's hustle is endless, my future undetermined.

Alejandra Rodriguez age 17

I am very proud of my parents, who are both Mexican immigrants, and my Mexican heritage. I dance folklórico *(a traditional Mexican dance), visit Mexico often and "dress like Frida Kahlo." As a result, assimilating into American culture and society is often difficult.*

Caught between Two Worlds

There is a well-known *corrido* called *"Jaula de oro,"* by Norteño group Los Tigres del Norte, in which a Mexican immigrant describes his life in the United States as similar to living in a cage made of gold. Because my parents are both Mexican immigrants, I grew up listening to this song and songs like it. It's one of my favorites. Yet I can't sing along to it because I "can't relate" to it — at least that's what my parents say.

I wasn't born in Mexico. I didn't go through the hardships of crossing the border, of leaving my country and family and life. I didn't feel the paralyzing fear of getting caught and deported. So how could I possibly relate to the struggle, they ask, if I was born with everything on a platter? Except, I don't feel like I belong here either.

Last summer, the other Junior Lifeguards weren't sure if I spoke English or not, because of my brown skin and black hair. At least they were polite enough not to ask, since others take it as an invitation to tell me to go back to Mexico. They call me *paisa* at school (sometimes a silky *rebozo* feels better than denim jeans) and *gringa* at home (I'm sorry for speaking Spanglish, *Mamita*, and I can't help it if my eyes water when I eat salsa, *Papi*).

Ni de aquí, ni de allá. Not from here, nor from there. It feels like I'm caught between two worlds, wishing I could just be me.

Make your writing as personal as possible.

Even if your subject matter

is worlds away from your everyday life

Zoe Frohna age 17

I wrote this monologue at the WriteGirl Character and Dialogue Workshop. The character is me (played by an actor), and the setting is the Linwood Dunn Theater where the workshop is held (very meta). I am using an actor to tell a story of mine.

Different Body, Same Mind

ZOE

I just switched bodies. My original body is somewhere in this audience. My original body has blonde hair, glasses and a wheelchair. And it's this last thing I switched bodies to talk to you about.

This is a monologue. I am this monologue.

(stretches)

This body is pretty cool. I like it. I like my original too, but ... I can't drive. My mom and I think I need a special car. And because I can't drive and because I have a huge (HUGE!) homework-related procrastination problem and require reminders to do things, I have a babysitter at age 16! Sure, she calls herself my "personal assistant," but what does that even mean? She assists me! And now you all think I need that! Guess what else I need? I'm in line to get a service dog in 2019. Which is great! It's mostly for companionship, and I LOVE dogs!

But what you don't know is, my mom won't let me take a walk with my chair or walker, or go anywhere on the Metro by myself. There always has to be a friend or a parent or a dog. I can't exist for myself until I'm an adult. I want to have my cinematic "teen" moment while I'm a teen!

(pauses, sighs)

Do you think that if I actually had the body of
(gestures to self)
[actual actor's name] I'd be better? No? Stronger? No. Freer? Maybe?

(bitter)
Do you think I'd be less awkward, and bold? Do you think I'd stop wishing people would NOTICE ME? Do you think I'd stop being loud? Do you think I'd stop FORCING YOU TO NOTICE ME?

I am what I am. I've gotten used to whatever the heck this is.

(angry)
I know my power. DO YOU?

Kiyanti Schlank age 17

For an English assignment, I was supposed to write about myself similarly to how a character in a novel did. However, creativity came along and threw me in a slightly different direction.

No Real Name

My name was scolded with looks of disappointment etched on faces and dragged places when I was a five-year-old who wanted to sing and draw and play instead.

My grandfather called me his hazel eyes, and I made memories in his album. My name was on applications and headshots, inked on paper with few lies when I was seven.

My name was the color of autumn leaves swirling in my line of fire.

My little brother had me named Cisi, short for sister. My creators called me Kiki. My name was both the slight frowns and smiles I received trying to heal pain but not always enough.

My name was who sang along to all the Disney songs. My friends called me slow, but also the one who always wears a smile.

My name caught grown-ups eyeing my little brother and me when we seemed lost and were alone. My name was Mulan.

My name was stereotypical cups of coffee, but who rarely consumes one cup a month.

My name was make-believe and stories embedded in my vault, my chamber, my mind.

My real name is ink, paper, thought.

DON'T EDIT AS YOU GO.

JUST WRITE,

WRITE,

WRITE

AND

EDIT WHEN YOU'RE DONE.

Sophia Rutt age 14

I wrote this song at the WriteGirl Songwriting Workshop. Lisa Loeb sang it during the performing part of the workshop. It was so cool to hear her sing my song onstage. I love singing, and I hope that someday I will be able to perform my original songs for a live audience.

Stuck in the Middle

Verse 1
She is always on the outside
She prefers to be alone
Always stuck in her artist world
Drawing superheroes

Pre-chorus
Then one cloudy morning, you step into her art class
Your eyes meet hers, but only for just a moment
She looks away, too shy to smile at you
What should she do?

Chorus
'Cause she's stuck in the middle
Stuck in the middle
Is this all just a riddle?
'Cause she's stuck in the middle
Stuck in the middle, not sure what to do

Verse 2
She likes you, but doesn't know if she should talk to you
You head in her direction
And sit down next to her
You think her artwork is beautiful
But you are not sure what to say

Chorus
You are stuck in the middle
Stuck in the middle
Is this all just a riddle?
You are stuck in the middle
Stuck in the middle, not sure what to do

Nicole Jefferson age 17

I wrote this poem to reflect on things that I wish that I knew when I was younger.

I Wish I Could Tell Her

I wish I could tell her
looking at the old photographs
when I didn't know so much
That girl with the sweet smile
and the *Dora the Explorer* backpack

I wish I could tell her
all the things to prepare for
Soccer practice in the neighborhood carpool
then driving yourself there in your mother's car
that she warned you not to scratch

I wish I could tell her
your score on your 10th-grade math final
won't matter; your worth is not determined by a number
Crying over that number is a waste of time
People care more about who you are

I wish I could tell her
all the feelings she will experience
Nerves, joy, frustration, disappointment, amazement
Remind her to be passionate and kind
even in moments of doubt

But if I did tell her,
her life wouldn't have been her own
to discover along the way,
and that would not be fair

Helen Graham age 17

This poem was inspired by the feeling of safety that being in a small space evokes.

Hide and Seek

There is freedom in darkness
It fills small spaces
So none is left for thoughts to creep in through my scalp and
I am no longer in my head
I am the eclectic fragments that escape out of both my ears
I am trapped in my skin pulled taut over broken bones and bruised belief
I am written all over my own face
I am spelled out completely across my forehead
And it's practically blank
Words scream through my hair
Begging for answers that shred me
Hands grasping to hang on
Smiles grind out from split lips
I must hide to find myself.

Lauren Thielen age 19

The title of this piece means "Not from here, nor from there." I wrote this when I was drafting essays for college admissions. I reflected on my past and tried to pull out what it means to be biracial.

Ni de aquí, ni de allá

I was eight years old when I first became aware of my background and the fact that I didn't quite resemble either of my parents. My mom is an immigrant from Mexico, and my dad has British-German ancestry. So that makes me a *chilaquile* — a blend of flavors, stuck in limbo between murky identities.

With every standardized test, I was forced to check a single box to illustrate my race and ethnicity. Was I considered "white"? But I'm a brown girl, so maybe I should have just checked "Latina" instead. There was no other option except to dissect my in-betweenness and confine it to small graphite boxes, and it reminded me of how society will view me as only a partial member of both groups.

I don't want to choose any longer. I am connected to both sides of my heritage and feel pride in knowing that I am wholly Xicana, British, German, American and Purépecha. I refuse to be put in a box.

Kayla Veloz age 16

People often tell me that I am too quiet and I should be more like others, but I tend to enjoy my solace. I experience more and understand others more when I am by myself.

My Bubble

My bubble is small
It slowly runs out of air
and I never speak to conserve what's left

My bubble is lone
It has space for only me
and it pops all those who come too close

My bubble is mine
It keeps me safe and free
and it allows me to float around endlessly

Emmett Thompson age 17

I wrote this poem about literally changing my name from my birth name to Emmett, and dealing with my depression and my place in this world.

no Name

my Name is not fear
not depression
or self doubt

i think of reasons to keep existing
breathing in and out
remembering each stutter
i have to count my fingers and toes
to make sure they haven't left me while I slept

i'm not scared
but i like to hide in dark corners
i look out of eyes of someone that isn't me
creating universes in everyone
i'm not small
in size
or in mindset
i go stargazing in the specks in my eyes
i see planets in my pupils

my Name is not misplaced
not random
or a waste

my Name is what I'm trying to find in the universe

Even if you don't think
it sounds good in your head,
just write it down.
It might turn out better
than you think.

2

Never More Than a Text Apart

Friendship

Culzean Giammatteo age 18

This piece is a response to an earlier poem I wrote for the last WriteGirl anthology, both of which are for Rileigh, my dearest friend. I love you, sis.

Space Bends for Us, Miles Mean Nothing

A year ago I wrote about mileage
Since you've been frozen in time, numbers have taken on a newer significance
I've started to think being human is giving significance to things that don't matter
like the cursive I keep inking into my skin —
song lyrics that meant something else to the artist

A year ago I wrote about missing you
Since I've been seeing bits of you, I've taken to tucking them into bits of me
I have your wrinkled nose beneath my bitten fingernails
your smile in the crease between my eyebrows
your upturned chin in the curve of my hip
It nudges me forward as I walk

A year ago I wrote about 31 days
Since then, it's gotten progressively harder to keep track
I'm sitting in a bathroom stall as I contemplate this
I find it helps to think of large things in small spaces
like you — infinite, stubborn, unyielding, large
You had to stop the world to give yourself a small enough space
to think

A year ago 31 seemed large
498 days, 9 hours and 12 minutes later
and the space between has finally compensated
A small space for a large thing

Natalie Mendez age 14

I wrote this poem because I wanted to show my endless gratitude to all of my incredible friends who have treated me so lovingly and kindly.

The Four Amigas

I want to thank you for all that you do
and to explain
what it means to have a friend
to share life's hardships and joys
It's good to know that our friendship is one of
endless loyalty
forged out of emotion and respect

It's patient and kind
never failing or forsaken
when a hand is outstretched
or one's heart is breaking

It's ever faithful
even when the world condemns
and sparkles in the darkness
like fireworks
It does my heart good
at the end of the day
to know that we will never be more than a text apart

Samantha Becaria age 14

This poem is about a friend who seems to be drifting away from me. I wrote it during the beginning of science class — the only class we have together — so that I could describe her. I remember her asking, "What are you doing?" and I just smiled at her.

"What Are You Doing?"

I was thinking of
          blue skies
sunsets
          rivers flowing
and how they remind me of you;

their beauty cannot be
          captured
by the skill of a pen,
          a brush on a board,
the flash of a camera;

just like how you cannot be
          contained by me,
my expectations,
          my faults;

feeling like I must hold you
          to keep you from
                    floating off.

Emily Tuckness-Kuntz age 17

In a never-changing town, Eren is a bored woman. But when a stranger blazes into her little world, Eren is changed for the better. This is an excerpt from my short story series called The Town.

Eren's Caramel Angel

The next hour and a half was a painful dedication to the stranger in silence. Eren's hands had been immaculately clean but were now tainted with graphite stains and a dull ache with the smell of the watercolor. The artist kept making adjustments, thinking that the piece wasn't right.

The caramel woman she drew and painted wasn't as brilliant as the one 10 feet away; the picture was missing a warmth she felt. And so tedious erasing and attentive movements went on to get the blend of her hair color just right and the folds in her massive sweater perfect.

But the woman gave no notice. She hardly moved. At one moment, it seemed Eren had a spectacular idea, and she made an excited effort to jot some notes down in the journal. Eren swore there was a halo glow painting a sunrise color around her figure in the drawing.

But in Eren's drawing, the woman was a shining citrine among pale and crude jaspers. Everything glistened: a corner of her mouth smiled slightly more than the other; stray pieces of frizzy hair she didn't make the effort to place back; fingers tapping in the same repetitive dance.

Eren tried to guess if she was playing an invisible instrument — a piano maybe? No, she only used three fingers. It was something smaller — maybe a woodwind? The citrine woman tapped while she was presumably thinking; she had a beautiful thinking face.

Annie Son age 16

"Drive" is actually my very first song written at the WriteGirl Songwriting Workshop. That morning, my childhood friend texted me for the first time in a while, and I wrote this song about missing her.

Drive

Verse
We run, run, free on the playground
Feet hangin' on monkey bars, we were just messin' around
After school we beg to sleep over
Separated, we could be never

Pre-chorus
Thirty miles
Sound of your voice lost through dials
Maybe when we finally get that car we always wanted
We can cross that border, get over it

Chorus
Drive, come home, my darlin' sis
We can't keep going on like this
Forget all life's problems, maybe
And drive to me

Sarah Carter age 13

I wrote this scene at the WriteGirl Character and Dialogue Workshop.

Rushing It

LILA and ASHLEY are in Lila's bedroom while she gets ready for a date.

LILA
I'm telling you, Ash, this is the one I was meant to be with for the rest of my life.

ASHLEY
Yeah, yeah. I've heard you say that about a million different men.

LILA
But this one is different. When I first saw him I was like when Juliet first laid her eyes on Romeo.

ASHLEY
Let me remind you that Romeo and Juliet ended in tragedy and this relationship won't be different than the others.

LILA
Come on, haven't you ever looked into someone's eyes and thought I wanna be with you for the rest of my life?

ASHLEY
Well, if you ask me, love is like all good things. It's gonna have to die at some point.

LILA
Well, this good thing is not going to die. I met him at the coffee shop and he was really nice and sweet.

ASHLEY

At least you didn't meet him on the street this time.

LILA

Hey, I didn't meet Dale on the street. I met him in a very dark alley.

ASHLEY

That's even worse! Look, I think you're trying to rush things.

LILA

What do you mean?

ASHLEY

Lila, when did you meet this guy?

LILA

Um ... yesterday.

ASHLEY

Wow, Lila, you really are something. Listen, you're the type of person who after the second date feels like you should be getting married.

LILA

What are you saying?

ASHLEY

I'm saying maybe you should cancel this date. I mean you only met him yesterday.

LILA

Maybe you're right. I must admit, I do often want to get into relationships fast.

ASHLEY

See? Now, when have I ever been wrong?

The DOORBELL rings.

LILA

Well, that's him.

Brandy Mendoza age 18

This was one of the first poems I wrote that made me realize I wanted to write for the rest of my life.

Will You Jump With Me?

Before, I was just on this train, waiting for it to take me away. I didn't care where — I just wanted to escape.

But then you joined the ride, and we became great friends. I knew I had to
get off at some point, but I stayed on this train to nowhere because of you.
I realized that I couldn't jump off without you.

So will you please jump with me? We could start a new journey together.
No matter where we go, I just want you by my side.

Hold my hand while we jump off this train that we once thought was useless but is now our path to a brand-new start.

Alyssa Ho age 14

I was inspired to write this piece at the WriteGirl Poetry Workshop in January. I was lucky to get Yazmin Monet Watkins as our workshop lead. She prompted us to write a "clapback" — a rant toward someone who wronged you. Then she told us to look on the opposite perspective and write about how you wronged someone else.

What I Regret Saying

What I regret saying:
Nothing.
Nothing.
I said nothing.
Absolutely nothing

When he pointed fingers at you
When he called you names
When he laughed at you
When he stole your glasses
When he hid your glasses
When he ruffled your hair
When he stroked your hair
When he pushed your shoulders
When he picked you up like his doll
When he wouldn't let you down
When he touched you.

I did nothing but sit
And pretend
That all that was happening was
Something you wanted.

I regret never saying something.

Taya Kendall age 17

In creative writing class, we do a "call of words" where our teacher reads a poem to us in hopes that a line sticks out and inspires a piece. I wrote this poem about my best friend.

Queen

an endless rhapsody
of blue and gold,
tired, electric eyes
light the way home.
her teardrops are dew
upon a burning rome
and if her kingdom's under siege,
she shuts it all down.
god's not real in her world;
it's her and her tigers and homer and mr. darcy,
all pantheonic and shimmering
with cobwebs and dust.

she spins her mouse-brown hair
white-gold and back again,
speaking in foreign tongues
and sometimes mine,
but always that of a harpsichord.
sometimes i fear commoners
will take her from me,
spray-paint her temple
and leave it muddy and bloody and raw —
but i know she worries the same of me.

california belongs to me
and sometimes her when she wants it.
i could never deny it to her.
not this, not anything.

Tell the stories
that you once needed to
hear/see.

We Step Forward

Growing Up

Kate Lewis age 14

I wrote this to showcase all of the millions of things that can lead to where you are, wherever you are.

All Those Times

All those times.
You can remember them like they were yesterday.

The time you walked into high school on your first day. Or maybe college.
The fights you endured as a child. The shattering of a plate against the wall.
Your first kiss. The first time you felt someone saw you, for you. Your first love.
Having to say goodbye to someone you loved. Looking at death right in the face.

First time seeing snow.
First time feeling blood trickle down your skin.
First time feeling not only butterflies but a whole zoo in your stomach.
First time you cried your heart out until you felt empty inside.

First time saying "You're dead to me" or "I love you"
and meaning it with every fiber of your being.
First time lying. Cheating. Stealing. Betraying.
First time walking down the aisle.

All of these things big or small led to where you are now.
Maybe standing in line for food. Or right outside of a job interview.

All of these seconds. Moments. Memories.
Led to this, to who you are.

Savannah House age 17

This piece was written shortly after I moved out of my childhood apartment while I was sitting at the pool, where I spent much of my summers as a child.

Unrecognizable Memories

I do not recognize this place
worn-down lawn chairs
black-dusted concrete floors
old, pale blue water.

We used to spend hours here as children.
I remember
perfectly clear water
a strong scent of chlorine
bright blue tiles not yet faded by sunlight and sunscreen
concrete floors clean of grout.

The words "I have lived here my whole life"
get caught in my throat — no longer true.
I can see my childhood home from here
if I just look up — and I do.

I half expect my dad to be home
grilling something delicious on the balcony.
I look across the way
expecting Alice to be smiling down at me
to tell me I have grown.
I expect the sun to come beaming through
and when I look down
I see myself in my popsicle one-piece — six years old again.

Pearl Dickson age 17

When you're going through hard times, sometimes it's hard to find empathy — whether for yourself, the world around you or something else entirely. This is why whenever I'm going through regular teenage angst, it's important to simply meet it in the middle.

The Ringer

Random acts of kindness from friends
seem rarer than the kindness of a stranger.
Lately, though, my cloud has cleared.
I've been put through the ringer but at last

I am at peace with it.
I've shaken hands with it
and thanked it
for the heartache it's made me feel.

The ringer is now my friend and we meet for lunch twice a week.

Sophia Moore age 16

This piece is addressed to my future self. It's a present promise that I'll make it to New York City and I'll accomplish my dream of living there to write. I love California, and it'll always be my home, but New York City is calling my name, and this piece is its response.

(The Things I Left Behind in) New York City

I've only been there once — so small standing among the fluorescent signs and tourist-trap buildings, so alive in the midst of all the sights and sounds. My heart and my head have been stuck in the skyscrapers; my body is grounded in California. The pseudo-glitz and glam doesn't compare to the rough edges of that fast-paced jungle; I need to go back.

My sights have been set far beyond the deserts and valleys of the Golden State; my future lies near the Atlantic. It longs for the bright gleam of Broadway musicals and the crisp cool of the winter. It beats for warm, hazy summer evenings in the park and walking anywhere my legs can carry me. The thing I think about most at night is this condensed city and its people and places; New York City has consumed my mind.

It's subtle, the ways that it influences me: Do a little bit better on a test — NYU and Columbia are watching. Think a little harder on where you want to vacation for the summer — Washington, D.C., is only four hours away. Bring it up to Mom and Dad once more — their hearts were stolen by this city once too. Every aspect of my life finds a way to make it about New York, and there's nothing California can do about it.

So goodbye to the Pacific beaches and too-warm weather, farewell to the spread-out cities and disunity in L.A., so long to the way Hollywood tries too hard to be something it's not. I'll be back someday. Hello to publishing houses and skyrise apartments, welcome to unglamorous living and romanticized dreams. My future is waiting for me 2,789 miles away, and I fully intend to find it.

Zoe Frohna age 17

I'm a wheelchair user. Sometimes I have energy to stand and walk or even go up some stairs. Sometimes I don't. This night I didn't.

Parties

The music feels like a punch in the chest.
The people prefer to remain strangers.
The snacks cramped in a room the size of a broom closet
(and bodies cramped in there too).

You were feeling like a cloud hovered over just you.
Second-guessed yourself the whole drive there
but decided,
"Yes! We're just going to watch a movie! I can just relax!"

Only to have that path blocked by a staircase,
and your cloud came back.

Not cloudy enough to leave.
Just cloudy enough that you can't get in.
When you're stunted,
you're
Stunted.

You don't want to be anyone else but you,
but it makes you wonder,
what it would be like
if parties were easy.

Cora Ries age 17

This is a personal monologue that I wrote about my childhood and the trouble I used to get into. I was a rather rambunctious and troublesome three-year-old, and I drove my parents crazy.

The Quiet Life

I went through my teenage rebellious phase when I was three. There was not a crib, baby gate or door in the world that could hold me. I was what one might call a *free* soul and I refused to be tied down, no matter how hard my parents tried — literally. When we would go camping, they had to resort to tying a blanket over the top of my crib to keep me in the tent and out of the adult beverages that people had left lying around.

I would sneak out of the house when I was supposed to be asleep for the night and totter into the alley. Mother was in tears when she finally found me, barefoot and dressed in a baby-pink pajama set, sitting in the mouth of our open garage.

My only response was, "I watch car go by." To this day I don't think she's gotten over it.

I have quieted down. I don't sneak out of the house at night to sit in alleyways or monkey my way over locked baby gates in the middle of the night to wreak havoc in the living room with my dinosaur figurines. I prefer the simpler undertakings of tea-drinking and novel-reading. I have *grown*, one might say. So now that my friends are going through similar phases, I can only laugh: I got there first.

Whenever an idea pops up,
write it down!
Don't let that
nugget go!

Ritika Kandarkar age 16

My feelings inspired me to write this song at the WriteGirl Songwriting Workshop.

Don't Give Up on Me

Verse 1
I smile, but no one knows if it's real or not.
I wish I could tell you what I thought.
The mask on my face won't stay up.
There are times I want you to shut up.

Pre-chorus
I walk through the hallways in a gray haze.
I know that I seem unfazed.
The walls around me are built so high.
It's because I'm scared, not because I'm shy.

Chorus
I scream and I cry.
Just please don't say goodbye.
Don't give up on me.
You think I'm a failure, don't you?
I gasp and I lie.
Baby, please don't say goodbye.
Don't give up on me.

Verse 2
I never used to be this way.
I think so many things, but none good enough to say.
I'm sorry that I'm so tightly shut.
Everything I think feels like a painful cut.

Chorus
I scream and I cry.
Just please don't say goodbye.
Don't give up on me.
You think I'm a failure, don't you?
I gasp and I lie.
Baby, please don't say goodbye.
Don't give up on me.

Write
what you

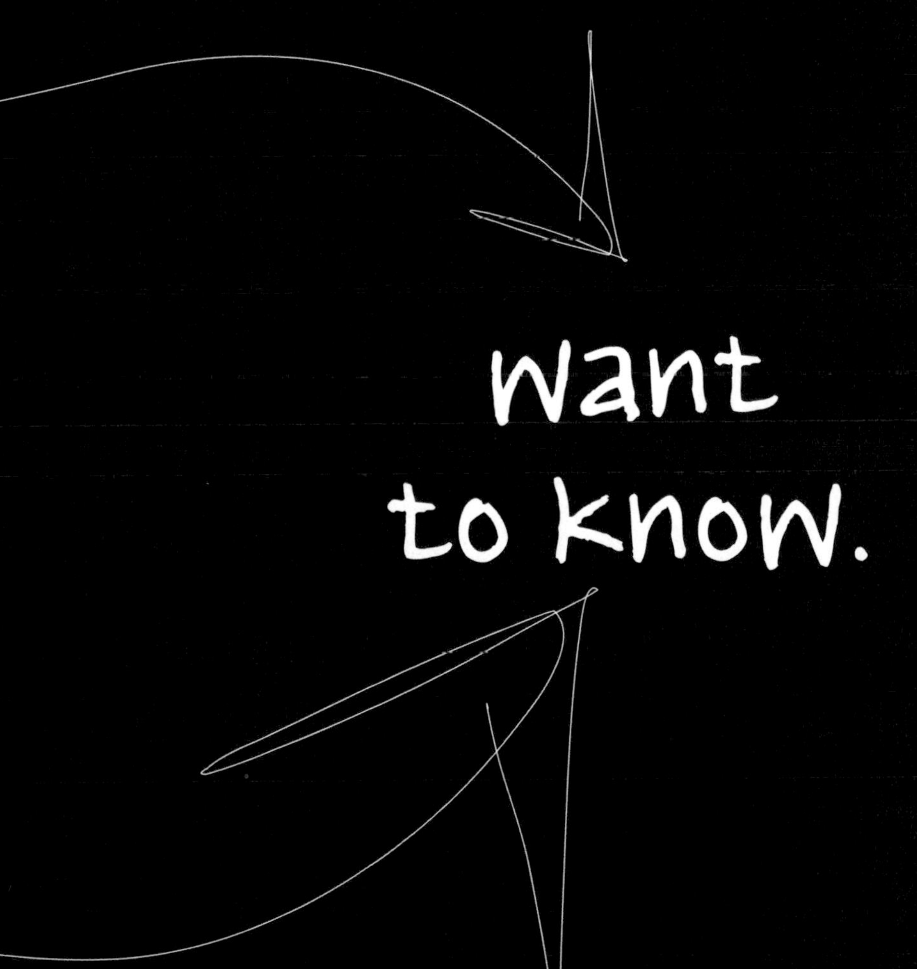

want
to know.

Jazzmin Joya age 14

I got inspired to write this poem while I was folding laundry and thinking about how almost all of my teddy bears are ripped or destroyed.

Eulogy to My Teddy Bears

Mrs. Pigsley, the first of them all
red thread engraved in your ear
my failed attempt to sew
no more tail
takes all the nightmares

Besssy, scaly friend
held together with safety pins
no more stuffing, but you're still here

Affie, my giraffe
a nickname became a spirit
the first boy in the group
you slept on the floor so many times

Eeyore, my pessimistic friend
memorabilia from a night out
you sit there and listen to my cries

Pepper Sunshine, a white-tailed fox
named by my sister who loved her at first sight
a Christmas gift, you fit right in
Love you all, best bed friends

Faiza Meah age 15

I wrote this piece after scrolling through Instagram and seeing racist posts. I was upset, and to deal with my anger in a healthy way I resorted to writing. This poem captures the essence of what it feels like to live in our world.

A World, a Sphere

We live in a world that's shaped like a sphere
We learn that in kindergarten, maybe first grade
We are taught that the world is bottomless
such as its oceans, its many bodies of water

We are taught to swim in our early years
to glide our arms up and over at a certain circumference
As we glide, we move our heads from side to side
We breathe
We are taught this and we listen

Why is it that we are taught science and evolution in kindergarten
but the science behind the beauty of others
and the evolution of the many different types of people —
that, that we are not taught
We must learn that on our own?

We are taught to swim in our early years
taught to glide left and right
But we still don't know what direction to follow
and we're no longer in the water

No, this is real life

Rhema Vincent age 14

I wrote this at the WriteGirl Songwriting Workshop.

My Pace

Verse 1
One after another they go
The more I see, the more I know
But I learn as I grow
I see the truth — it always shows

Pre-chorus
I don't really know
How this happens
But I know that this is my chance
I reminisce a sequence from the past
Step back, take a glance

Chorus
I guess it's just another
Opportunity gone to waste
But I'm learning
At my own pace

Culzean Giammatteo age 18

This piece was inspired by a list of words that describe very specific but universal feelings, and the end of an era.

Graduation

Resfeber (n.): the restless race of the traveler's heart before the
journey begins, when anxiety and anticipation are tangled together

A series of uncomfortable chairs and bureaucratic goose chases
have brought me here
The final uncomfortable seat of the era
The end of my transition

This place feels smaller without my former peers
or perhaps I'm just bigger now
Squares dance in the air as we chase the fleeting moments
before finality sets in

Now back to the very first square
We built the ground — we just have to build up
Adventure and terror lie at our feet
We step forward

Coddiwomple (v.): to travel in a purposeful manner toward a
vague destination

Read It Out Loud

News & Society

Sophie Rosenblum age 16

When I read Lori Alhadeff's letter, written one year after her daughter was lost in the Parkland shooting, I was inspired to write. As a student and a girl who is very close with her mother, this letter impacted me deeply. While her daughter can't send a response, mine is below.

From Another Daughter

I read your letter in my bed, with a clay mask hardening on my face. A one-sided conversation between a mother and her daughter that I got to listen in on. I stumbled upon it after scrolling through Instagram mindlessly — a habit that your daughter Alyssa may have experienced but now can't. Your words overwhelmed me with gratitude. I'm not the recipient of the letter — I'm a girl reading it from the comfort of her own bed.

You talk about how things have changed since that Valentine's Day, a day that started off with red fuzzy animals and pink bows, and quickly drained of color. One year later, color is seeping into your life, but Alyssa's sparkle won't return.

"I wish I could take all the bullets for you." When I read that line, I crumbled like the clay on my face, disrupted by streaming tears. From the kitchen, I heard my mom making dinner and imagined her taking all the bullets for me. She would do it an instant.

The next morning I begged her to read your letter. She was busy; I read it out loud. Your words were the background noise to her bustling morning, but they slowly weighed her down until I found our eyes locked, her body held up by one rigid arm leaning over the countertop. By the time I reached the bullet line, we found ourselves crying over cereal.

Mrs. Alhadeff, as poignant and meaningful as your letter is, I never want to read one similar again. I have no interest in living in a world where parents live with trepidation when they drop their children off at school. I'm tired of planning escape routes and hiding places. Let's live for a future where school and fear aren't so deeply interwoven. Until that day, I will remember your letter and appreciate every breakfast with my mom.

Gianna Garcia age 15

I know that one day I will be a successful something. Now, do I know what that "something" is? No. However, I do know that it will involve copious amounts of work to help lower-income families because that is what makes me fired up.

La Pauvreté

The sound of the bells on that morning,
never-ending feelings of warmth.
Filling their stomachs with macaroons,
knowing that tomorrow there shall be more.
Others aren't so lucky.
They've never experienced the warmth
of biting into a crunchy croissant on an early morning.

Chloë Mirijanian age 17

This poem was inspired by the sight of Omran Daqneesh, a child featured on the news a while back because of his stupefied and bloodied face after suffering from an airstrike in his hometown of Aleppo.

The Do's and Don'ts for Wartime Massacres

1. DO rip out your heart.
Emotions will take over. And you must have none.
A stone, ceiling, picture frame, a drawer.
Think of something inanimate. Become it.

2. DON'T have a brain.
It can make you think critically.
The very fibers and folds of the hemispheres of your mind
must be destroyed.

3. DO be systematic.
Become one with your weapon and fire.
You are a machine.
An automatic, destructive, fierce, ferocious, aggressive monster
with an appetite for demolition.

4. DON'T look at them.
Never look into their eyes.
They will stop your mission, kill your game.
Like a blade, they will slice you up with those terrified windows to the soul.
Their arms are raised, at your mercy; they are children.
But they will still ravage you harder than you will the city
with your bombs, guns, grenades.

5. DON'T look at the mothers.
Ignore the trembling hands, the weeping eyes.
The crouched back, the shaking and screaming voice.

Don't.

Maria Guinnip age 16

I wrote this poem when two schools right next to mine experienced gun violence in only one week. I was very shaken and angry, and this was how I expressed my feelings.

A Terrible Template

To my right, students stare at school walls
stained with threats,
terrified of what's to come.
Administration does nothing.

To my left, students sprint in search of cover —
a student falls,
a teacher falls
in a crosswalk just outside school walls.
A bullet now encased in the flesh
of a boy who once loved to skate.
Administration does nothing.

Students protest.
Parents won't rest.
Administration brushes it aside.

People protest.
States won't rest.
Government brushes it aside.

Satiated thoughts and prayers
as if they follow some template.
Just change the school, change the date.
Why can't we change their fate?

Write with a purpose.

Jacqueline Alvarez age 17

I wrote this after listening to a case where a man was wrongfully incriminated.

Guilty

July 7, 2016.
Marie Andrews is found dead in her home.
You
are on her front porch camera —
the only person to have entered her home that day,
her blood on your clothing.

"Tell me, Paul. I want to know.
(fluorescent lights buzzing)
You claim you aren't guilty. I hear you.
But the evidence is pitted against you.
Especially your past."

October 14, 2005.
The day your mother was found dead.
Your fingerprints on the gun.
The only person she was with
before she was found.

"The decision has been made.
The facts
speak for themselves."

(a clock strikes 6 p.m.)
(silence)

Gillian Chamberlin age 14

I wrote this piece to represent how a person can become so weighed down by being abandoned.

The Bathtub

A woman sat by a bathtub, knees tucked up to her chest, fingers absently swishing in the warm water. Her frizzy, dark hair was down on her shoulders. She seemed almost too young to be a mother, but the way the baby in the tub grabbed at her hands showed a connection that could only be maternal. The stiff and moldy shower curtain hung bunched behind her head.

She stared at the wall, counting the tiles. She wore an oversized T-shirt with cracking white Hawaiian flowers on it, her hair unsuccessfully pushed behind her ears, her hand in the cooling water, her fluttering baby in the tub.

A chubby hand splashed in the water. Each finger was like a small breakfast sausage, so plump and round at the joints. So pure that if you were blessed by those small fingers clutching at your T-shirt or hair, even if they had slobber on them you would let them continue with their exploration.

The baby was up to his waist in the cyan bath water. Rubber ducks in cowboy hats bobbed around him. Colorful styrofoam letters stuck to the side of the bathtub spelled out gibberish.

The bathroom windows were fogged; necklaces hung on the latches of the windows; golden earrings sat in disorganized piles on the sill.

The jangled ring of the telephone threaded down the hallway like ink through water. The ring called her across the stained wooden floor, splinters stuck into the calluses on her well-worked feet.

Sabina Garcia age 17

This piece is an excerpt from a novel that I've been writing off and on for about three years now. This scene is where the main character finally allows her boyfriend to meet her best friend, only he's in for a surprise.

Let's Meet Angel

After so much pestering, Domnus finally convinced me to introduce him to Angel.

"Heh, she's gonna be shocked," I thought as I prepared a picnic *cesta*.

When he picked me up to go visit her, he began asking me where to go. "Just follow my directions," I said. After 30 minutes, we finally arrived at our destination. I got out and said, "Follow me" and began *caminando* up a hill.

When I stopped, I smiled and said to my friend, "Hey, we haven't talked in a while. It's so weird, right? We used to talk every day. Anyway, I brought your favorites. Oh! And you'll never believe this, but my idiot of a twin *hermano* finally got a *novia*! I give them a week, and you?"

"Um, Flori, what are you doing?" Domnus asked.

I took a deep breath and moved aside to show him the beautiful grave. "Domnus, meet Amethyst Williams, or Angel as *todo el mundo* refers to her."

Domnus was shocked. "Wait, I thought you said she moved to Spain."

"No, I said her *familia* moved to Spain. Angel never left." I began to tear up. "She's forever 14."

"If you don't mind me asking, how did she die?"

"She's one of the victims of the Diana Perez Middle School shooting."

"Oh my God."

Domnus hugged me as my eyes overflowed with tears.

Ask the question:

What do I want people to learn from this story or scene?

Olivia Calderon age 17

This poem is about climate change. We are looking at a future of the Earth taking back its land if we don't make a change now.

The Earth Is Not Flat

Mother mountain promises man a stone.
Mother mountain calls to Sister storm.
Nature eroding Mother mountain's throne.

Man grows a vile thing.

Mother Earth, she howls, despair in the air.
Father fire hears her desire.
She roars, dooming mankind's soul.
Volcano erupts.

Mother mountain's throne reclaims her stones.

Alana Washington age 16

The idea for this came to me when I was watching the news and something about police brutality movements popped on the screen.

No Place Like Home

Lying awake at night
the whirl of helicopters
a bedtime story
Do you hear them?
I mean, where you're from,
do you hear them?
Stories of this place I call home
being twisted
It's dangerous out there, they say
Nothing good comes out of there
But this is home
That boy in the streets
my brother
That hard-working woman
my mother
And me

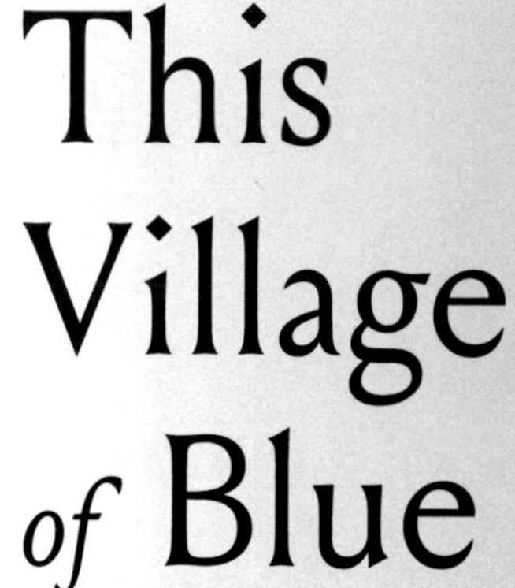

This Village of Blue

Colors

Allyson Roche age 17

My best friend Nikki passed away before I took this drive, and it was an event that changed my life.

The Odyssey

The grays and greens of the 101 create a hybrid of beauty and pain, the hills the shade of an ugly crayon that no child colors with. I feel my maroon dress hitting my leathery, worn boots that are too familiar to my feet. I've experienced this before, but it's as if I'm seeing everything through new eyes. I remember my ribs aching from cackling with Nikki. My heart now aches because I want to share another laugh with her.

A year later, I sit in a different car, in the same shoes, on the same drive, hearing the same song, in the same spot in Los Angeles. I stick my head out of the window not to see, but to feel the Crucifix and the Hollywood Sign that I've passed by countless times before yet failed to interact with. The lights of the city overshadow the dark silence of the freeway and the music is too loud to feel on the outside; it's only playing in my head.

I thrust my fist out of the window, and I feel the wind through my fingers. I'm jolted back by the unexpected power of the wind, but I challenge it. I push my hand against the air, allowing the infinitesimal troubles to escape from my chilled fingertips. I can see the past year like a queen on her throne viewing her kingdom, remembering the changes that were made and contemplating the changes yet to come.

The royal trumpets fill the air, their volume adding life to the wind. I feel content in this seat. I feel peaceful in this seat. The song is at its end, but I am only starting.

Addissyn House age 18

I picked up this piece a year and a half after writing it. With the help of my mentor, I distilled the longer poem into something more potent and more of the me that had grown up a little bit.

We Crossed the County Line Last Night

I wake up to midnight city lights still looking for the Big Dipper
  lost when we crossed the county line
I am all shades of ocean, especially the snarling blue-gray of the storm
I am half-awake death, alive with brightly colored bees and loneliness,
my mother's soft country drawl and my father's nasally northern accent
  on only some words
I fall asleep thinking of California rain on faded jeans
  asking, remember me?
I am afternoon walks in autumn's crisp early winter breeze on the wrong coast,
the old couch we're too attached to to get rid of
  remember me?

Liberty Macias age 16

I wrote this as a goodbye to my childhood. It's based on real memories I have of when I was younger.

Orange Peels

Orange peels
Scattered on the ground
Like a puzzle
We try to put back together
"It's okay; they'll decompose."

Wind tangling our hair
Hot faces meet cool air
Avoid the cracks on the sidewalk
"Where's my scooter?"

Yellow flowers
Sniffing jasmines
Sucking passion flower fruit seeds
"They look like brains."

The sun is barely present
I can see the moon
"Fifteen more minutes!"

Where did our time go
How did the years fly
Let's go back to wondering
What it'd be like to be older
The orange peels have decomposed.

Eva Brewster age 13

This poem is about a colorful sunset on the beach. It was inspired by a rose called "Royal Sunset" I saw at The Huntington during a WriteGirl workshop.

Crown of Gold

I drift to sleep
Then to blue
I watch as Mother Earth paints the black sky pink
The pink sky fades to orange
White light where the stars should be
The moon wakes up, though the stars don't sing
I lay there until the sky is empty of the colorful reflection
Orange, purple, pink
Drops of color in the darkening sky
When I wake, the sun wakes too
She wears a new crown of gold
Beach towels soft as the warm summer sand

Don't be afraid to write
from a perspective
different from your own.
Great writing asks
great questions.

Cristal Rincon age 16

When I think of the future, all I wish for is happiness.

Goodbye

I have spent too long wasting,
somber and silenced in this village of blue.
These streets have marked
streaks of cyan upon my swollen cheeks.
Cerulean has leaked into the cracks on my tongue,
until every syllable I spoke became a shade of anxiety.
Iris followed heartbreak and dusted my skin azure.
It's time I wash the canvas free of this melancholy.

All that's left to say now is goodbye.
Goodbye to worried mothers,
to my dad's tense shoulders,
to the armor my sister wears.
Goodbye to broken glass,
to the numbness in my hands,
to the screaming bouncing off the walls in my mind.

You say goodbye to close friends,
to relatives you know you'll see again.
But how do you say goodbye
to the blue that's become a part of you?

Jane Han age 13

This piece is inspired by one of the things that I love: art. The poem tells how I feel whenever creating art or getting inspired by it.

Stories

Swirls of colors
rising together to show me a story.
One painted in red
draped in blue.
Tales of the living.
Tales of the dead.
All with their stories to tell
and tell it they will,
on a canvas
as vast
and limitless as time.

Zoe Jean-Sprecher age 16

I wrote this poem for my mémère *(grandmother), who asks that the presents I give her be recollections of memories, whether in the form of writing, drawing or something else.*

A Memory to My Mémère

Winding Road.

To my left, the cliffs fall away to the sea.
Bright and brilliant are the blues of its water.
The foaming surf meeting rock and sand
and spots of the sea's surface.
Both shine white in the sun's light.

It seemingly stretches on forever,
seamlessly becoming sky
of the same blue
with clouds
of the same white.

To my right, the cliffs become smooth sprawling mountains
and valleys of green.
Redwoods dot the cliffs
and fill the valleys and mountains.

To my left, the sea will extend till the Land of the Rising Sun.
To my right, the land will sweep till the sea of the Atlantic.
A vast expanse of sea, a vast expanse of land.

Devon Bryce age 14

When I wake up, sometimes I hate the sun. It's too bright. But I decided to use it as a metaphor for that person who is always too bubbly and cheerful. You need that person around.

Good Morning

good morning, sun
you smile at me
with your rays

tell me to wake up
to smell the flowers
to feel the wind

see the crystal sky
filled with pinks
and oranges and blues

sipping oolong tea
and listening to the birds
I feel happy

so thank you, sun
for telling me to wake up
and enjoy each day
as if it were my last

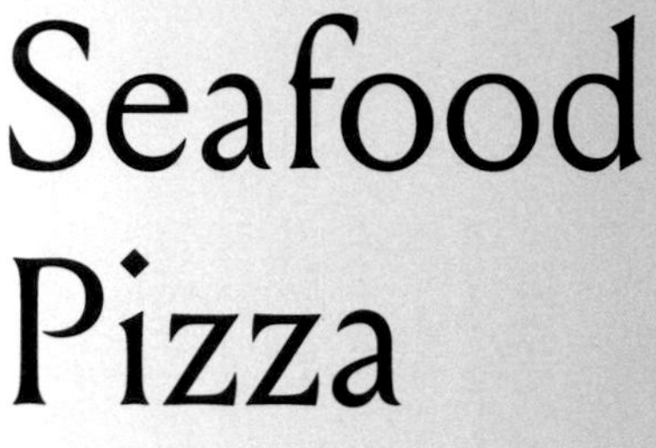

Seafood Pizza *with* My Cousins

Home

Bibiana Mashamba age 19

This piece was inspired by a beautiful place I lived growing up near Lake Victoria.

Kastamu

The yellow pipe stretched from one village to another,
water from Lake Victoria streaming down from it like a storm.

People washed and dried their clothes
and children like me bathed right there in public like it was one of our games.
Fishermen stretched the nets off their boats
and sang lullabies for the fish to sleep dead in them.

Sometimes when the water was as clear as a crystal,
big ferries would come and children would climb on them.
You could see the fish swimming down on the sand bottom chasing each other,
the sand so orange as if reflecting the sunset.

Makena Ababon age 16

During the holidays, I took my first international trip to visit my grandmother in Vietnam. Instead of appreciating Vietnam, I was anxious to return home. Upon arriving in Los Angeles, I realized the true purpose of traveling to Vietnam was not to enjoy a luxurious vacation but to spend quality time with my bà ngoOi *(grandmother).*

Homesick

Nineteen-hour flight.
No air conditioning.
Children beg for money.
Mosquitoes carry malaria.
I miss home.
Taxis don't have seatbelts.
My hair grows with the heat.
Strangers claim to be family.
I miss home.
Grandma cries at the gravesite.
Stray dogs viciously bark at me.
My family doesn't speak English.
Middle seat between stinky travelers.
I miss home.

Seafood pizza with my cousins.
My grandmother's cooking.
Beautiful marble graves.
Marley wagging her tail.
I miss Vietnam.
Getting Thai massages.
Coffee at Mikun Town.
Buying leather boots.
My *bà ngo i*.
I miss Vietnam.

Listen everywhere to hear
all the different kinds of dialogue
and ways to speak.

Phoebe Perkins age 16

I was inspired to write this piece at a WriteGirl workshop where one of the guest speakers taught us about poetry of place, and I decided to write about San Antonio, Texas, where my mom's side of the family lives.

July Rain

I can still smell the river, dominating all my senses with its rough, almost severe smell; not bad, not good, just home.

I can feel the humidity cling to my skin as I drive past the brightly colored homes, each one bigger than the last, giving me the feeling of a simpler time.

I can still see the sunny sky fill with clouds almost instantly as the hot rain turns a classically beautiful day into my kind of beautiful day.

I can hear the monstrous thunder, frightening the children and golden retrievers scattered throughout the house.

I can still picture the lightning illuminating the sky like a stage light, too bright — an artificial sun. The gray clouds fade into one another as the sound of wind chimes, the sound of familiarity, is picked up by the growing wind ... and suddenly it is over.

Ariana Cortez age 18

I wrote this piece when I first entered my freshman year of college and experienced the ignorance of others who don't appreciate Mexican culture and look down upon it. I also wrote this piece for myself and my family, to never forget our heritage.

Mexico Querido

I am from *chanclas y cinturones*
From overflowing pots full of brown beans
I am from *chilaquiles* and burnt tongues
From 2 a.m. parties and loud drums
Pulling each other's hair and cakes smashed into faces
From dark alleys and well-lit houses
Avena and *arroz con leche* steaming in the pot
From bruises and cuts, and the warm hands of my *abuelita*
saying, *"Sana sana colita de rana"**
From large blankets with lions imprinted on the front
Braids that always came undone
Lemon trees basking in the sun
Aguas frescas that dance around on my tongue
From rough labored hands that lit candles when things got rough
From Yaqui heritage and Aztec blood
And strong family bonds that can never be struck

*"Heal, heal little tail of the frog"

Marie Sekiguchi age 14

When I was writing this piece, I was at a lighthouse — not exactly a clock tower but close enough to remind me of one — and listening to a song called "Kaleidoscope."

Kaleidoscope

Carolyn was packing to leave the ancient clock tower that she'd lived in and loved for so long. A knock came at her old metal door, and she ran over to open it for her father. He smiled to see her young face framed by beautiful sandy-blonde hair, her light blue eyes that complemented her brown travel gown.

Carolyn's eyes filled with sorrow as she saw a tear streak down her father's wrinkly face. He put on his glasses. They teetered at the rim of his stiff nose.

"I need to show you something."

Tucking his hands into the pockets of his trench coat, he turned away. She reached for his hand. They walked silently up the spiral staircase, toward the back of the clock. Carolyn had never been allowed up there, but she was too busy staring at the steps in front of her, hiding her watery eyes.

Finally, when they reached the top, she found herself gazing at shooting stars. But they were coming out of thin air — no, from outside the clock's glass.

"Oh Papa, I —" she began in a cracked voice. He shushed her, letting her head lay on his shoulder. They were together this last time, and that was all that mattered. They watched the night sky turn and fall like a kaleidoscope.

Tindi Mashamba age 19

I wrote this poem in 2017 to express how much I miss home. Emily Dickinson inspired me to write this poem.

I Want to Go Home

I want to go home
Home to find my mom and dad
Home to see my brother and sister
I want to go home

Home where I play with my favorite toys
Home where they cook my favorite foods
Home where I have my own room
I want to go home

Home where I feel safe and comfortable
Home where there is no sorrow but happiness
Home where there is no judgment
I want to go home

Home where I was born
Home where I feel I belong
Home where they know my name
I want to go home

Lucy Eller age 18

This is a shortened version of the prologue to a novel-in-progress titled Charlie. *I wondered, "Is it possible to write a story with a third-person narrator who is an active, conscious voice — and a participating character?" The purpose of this specific piece is to establish context — where the story takes place, what can be expected and, of course, the voice of the narrator.*

Opening Statement

Our story takes place in the town of Winwood, Massachusetts. It's a sweet, idyllic town, fairly small in size. To the east, there's the beach, and to the west, the forest, where there are hiking trails and delightful campsites, if you're the type who likes to rough it. And the town itself? Postcard-worthy.

I'm sure that now you're expecting me to launch into some long-winded description of Winwood and its delightful townspeople, all the while hinting at some "hidden darkness" beneath its façade of "children's book suburbia."

You're clearly a smart one, aren't you?

But I'm not going to try and convince you that Winwood is just as innocent as it appears and gradually reveal its "secret shadows" as some huge plot twist. I would never put you through that, my darling.

So I'll tell you right now: Winwood's appearance isn't the truth of it and never was. It's a town of secrets, lies, abuse, murder, suicide, madness, witchcraft and more. Much, much more. There are indescribably horrific things in Winwood. Universe-destroying, mind-breaking, all-powerful things. Though I'm sure you knew that from the moment I called it "idyllic," didn't you?

I can tell you want me to stop droning on so you can get to the good stuff. But there's one last question I'm sure you have: Who am I?

That's a very, very good question. But I'm going to remain unnamed for now. Though I'm sure you knew that too. Don't worry, my smart cookie. You'll see me again very soon. Here's a hint: I'm not just the omniscient narrator.

Now let's begin at the only place we can: the inciting incident — the day a new girl moved in, a wounded man was found rambling to himself in the woods, and Misty Nolan died.

Twice.

Chloë Vigil age 18

College can be a big and confusing place, needless to say, and this poem came from the uncertainty and chaos that I was feeling.

First Semester

the rat scratches the inside of my tv screen
rabbit antennae stand at attention
when you kick in my door,
a flurry of white envelopes cover the floor,
more convenient than carpet.

home
has static in the windows and
paints chips lining the bathroom sink,
plumber drumming on the brain I keep in my closet.
move everything three inches to the left and
try to find myself
again.

Marilyn Marroquin age 16

My inspiration for this poem was eating pan dulce *and the saying, "The little things matter."*

A Piece of Me

Pan dulce for Sunday breakfast
12 a.m. conversations with Mom
Coffee with just enough sugar, bittersweet
Like my life, evolving

A home with walls painted
By the colorful souls it is filled with
As our bodies danced with the rhythm of a guitar
We made sure to paint others' lives

The world was black and white
I'm a sunflower
A seed from a thick stem
That bloomed to a bowl of happiness

As the ones with hatred in their eyes whispered, "grow up"
I am the beauty in destruction
Life is a pattern of art
Good to bad to the worst for the better

When the Light Flickers

Impermanence

7

Mia Swanson age 14

I wrote this piece while in the hospital for a few days after a frightening medical experience. It was my way of saying that the recent past may have been filled with darkness and sadness and that I'm still trying to find the light, but that I should always look forward to tomorrow and the future.

Rising Flames

Yesterday left ash.

Today revives fallen flames.
Hopes and dreams fuel the fire.

Soot black when the light flickers.
Flares again much brighter now.

Tomorrow shines light.

Sequoia Sherriff age 18

After my grandfather died, my mother hung the blue roses from his funeral up in my bathroom, and every time I saw them, they broke my heart just a little more.

Blue Roses

Blue roses drying in the bathroom. Ones with stems once so full of life now hang shrunken, above their withered buds, dyed blue. Tied upside-down to a lopsided white plastic hanger, with twine from my mother's bottom kitchen drawer.

Three weeks, my mother said. Three weeks of waiting for the delicate and gorgeous blooms to dwindle and perish.

Two weeks ago, I had been desperate to see those flowers vanish. I had done my fair share of sobbing a copy of my own face into my pillow at night. Glancing in the bathroom mirror, seeing red-stained eyes. Patience held me back with a gentle, soothing hand, one that offered tissues and repeated delicate circles against my spine.

One week ago, fury rose in me like a tidal wave, threatened to consume everything in its path. My muscles tingled with rage. I wanted to rip the dwindling blooms from their delicate strings and crush them. Destroy them until they were nothing but crumbles of blue-tinged ash.

This week I have no more tears to shed, no more anger in my veins. This week, I just miss you. I miss you so much that the air feels heavy around me, empty yet full of loneliness. I miss you so much that the world seems drained of color. So much it's indescribable. The funeral passed like a blur, leaving me nothing but scrunched-up tissues in my peacoat pocket, a black dress hanging limply over my cat-hair covered chair and blue roses politely dangling in my bathroom.

Valerie Chavez age 19

I wrote this piece while I was going through my last year of high school. With plans to move out for college, I described the sentiments of finishing my last year and compared it to the changing seasons.

Changing Seasons

When the cherry blossoms wrinkle with time
Sing to the heavens about fleeting youth
Make the stars promises you can't keep
Rest in the clouds of dreams with happy endings

When the leaves paint themselves beautiful colors
Yell to the moon your honest prayers
Rant to the sky that you can no longer take it
Fight the blind peace threatening to take over your eyes

When the snowflakes can no longer sustain their shape in this crowded world
Lament to the earth beneath you about fleeting youth
Remember your selfishness as you tried to grasp freedom
Let regret be the only feeling you leave behind

Just keep writing.
And look outside romantic relationships for material,

at least sometimes.

Eden Hirsch age 14

This short film script starts out as a monologue about how alone one ghost girl feels but turns into a conversation about how much of an impact she actually had. I initially wrote it during free time during a WriteGirl workshop, but my mentor helped me finalize the perspective and meaning of the excerpt.

The Invisible Girl

EXT. SCHOOL - DAY

JULIA PEABODY (15, dusty blonde ponytail, large square glasses and pale skin with freckles) stands at the main steps in front of her school, grimacing. She's watching a group of girls laughing with each other. She scowls as she walks past them and away from the school.

EXT. SUBURBAN STREET - DAY

Julia walks down the street and begins talking to herself.

JULIA

It already feels like I've been dead forever now. I have been 15 for the past three months, I think? I was trying to communicate with my mom at my funeral. I've always been invisible, in both life and death. I knocked all those stupid plastic chairs over, hoping that she would feel my presence. But I didn't even get a stupid cliché line like, "Oh I can still feel her presence!" Nothing. Nada. Zilch. You know what? I'm glad I'm dead, no one listens to me anyways.

Julia stops and looks down. The camera tilts — she's looking at a dead crow. We reveal that her legs fade from visibility at the knee like a ghost. Julia crouches and begins talking to the crow.

JULIA (CONT'D)

In school I was always a major wallflower, not by my fault of course. If someone tried to talk to me I would be happy to be their friend, but being that I'm in high school, everyone has their clique that they stick with. They probably don't even notice that I'm gone.

Julia stands up and continues forward.

JULIA (CONT'D)

Sometimes I see a boy who's in some of my classes waving to me, but then I look behind me and there's someone waving back. Even if I do wave, it's not like it matters. Being a ghost means I'm invisible to everyone —

LUKE (O.S.)

Hey Jules, are you good?

Julia's eyes go wide. She spins around to see LUKE MYERS (16, dark brown hair with tan skin and kind, hazel eyes; he's wearing Adidas sweatpants and a Thrasher hoodie, backpack slung over one shoulder). Luke is looking directly in her eyes.

JULIA

Wait, you can see me?

LUKE

I always see you.

Macy Kwon age 15

This piece was inspired by personal events and was meant to be therapy.

Tumor

When the pain comes in waves
and blankness is a common friend,
the grasps upon the broken ties of slithers of feeling
are lost once again.
Life moves on in swirls of moments and shouting,
while time stops in a prison of soundless hurting.
Voice stolen.
Wasn't it just yesterday ...
As the light shines from outside, here hidden I lie,
in the shadows of a curtain.

Colette Rogers age 13

This is simply a piece about the love between a father and daughter. The loss of a parent is heartbreaking, especially when the two of you shared an experience. I wanted to write this piece to touch the hearts of others who may have lost a loved one.

Iris

Willow's father would take her on trips around the harbor, where her locks would blow in the wind and occasionally dip into the crystal waters. Her father's grin was made out of jewels and crisp mouthwash. Their kayak was the color of stale coffee engraved with Willow's initials, carved when she was five.

Her father's sunspots and long eyelashes were permanently stuck in her memory. She wished she could still smell the seafood in the wind of the harbor's hush. They named that kayak *Iris*, the name of Willow's favorite character in a children's book.

Her father would tuck her in and whisper the same three words: *You're my light.* Hues of oranges and pinks matched his rosy cheeks. Willow prayed at night saying, *You're my light, Papa.*

She knew he was still in the kayak — his soul, his spirit. At 4 a.m., Willow woke and found herself inside *Iris*. She felt the sunbeams bathe her as she could feel her father's arms around her.

She looked at her beachside house and saw it burnt to the ground. Many died that night from a forest flame, but her father's spirit saved her — he led her to *Iris*. Her one memorial of the sunny days became a chair facing the flames.

Sofía Salazar age 17

I was listening to a piano cover of Adam Lambert's song "Outlaws of Love."

War

Verse
On the battlefield breathing in the cold
Your bittersweet kiss haunts my soul
On the battlefield last time we were here
Face to face we destroyed this place

Chorus
Oh we've started a war
That will never ever end
Oh we've started a war
This is a wound we cannot mend
Oh we've started a war
That's tearing me apart
Oh we've started a war
That's breaking my heart
Oh-oh oh-oh
That's breaking my heart

Hana Saadi-Klein age 16

I wrote this memoir about the first time I realized life's impermanence.

Tinted Gray

I stared up at beige walls, dimly lit by fluorescents. Grandma — silk hijab covering her hair, long skirt billowing — enveloped me in the familiar sweet smell of her perfume, chattering in excited tones of Farsi I couldn't comprehend. Something was missing — the twinkle that had always shone in the blue depths of her eyes was gone, as if the Northern Star had been ripped from the sky. It scared me, that lack of light, the absence of happiness.

I took her hand. "Let's go see him."

I was used to Grandpa — tall, strong-yet-gentle, deep rumbling voice — when the creases on his face were scars of laughter, not age. Now, he lay in bed, small and frail, drained of all his color and warmth. I couldn't recognize him. I bent over to hug someone who felt like a distant acquaintance.

The smell of sickness and chemicals mixed with perfume suffocated me. I tried to inhale but no air lived in this room. I couldn't breathe. Tasting the salt and shame on my tongue, I fled, tears streaming as I ran down the hall. I found solace behind a column, glimpsing my wretched face reflected in the vent overhead — my gasping mouth, my matted hair plastered to sticky cheeks. Everything was tinted gray.

It was then I thought, how colorless fear is, until it possesses something, paralyzing every other emotion. It leaves the body unwanted, letting loving arms scoop up the broken and the weak.

Lily Mead age 14

I wrote this based on my mom. I picked the one thing that has affected me the most in my childhood and how I learned to deal with it.

The Change

Walking home from my second-grade class every day
through my old red door, I started to notice a big change.
Something began to feel off. My mom had started to change.
She hadn't been coming around as much as before.
Once her MS got bad, my life went downhill.
I was seven.

I still didn't know why this had to happen to me.
I wondered why my friends' moms could do everything.
Some nights I would lie as straight as a ruler and just think.
I was only nine.

I finally started to understand. I realized that this was my life now
and I still loved my mom more than anything.
I would come home from school every day and pray.
Pray that everything would change and she would be healthy again.
I truly believed that it would all go my way.
I was 11.

After growing up even more, I learned that this was now my life.
I was done hoping and praying for it all to change.
I learned to help out and become my best self.
I was finally able to go to sleep not feeling worried.
I was finally 14.

Don't limit yourself to genres you already know.

The wealth of your own human experience is enough to fuel writing of any kind.

Balms & Powders

Image

Faith Alm-Clark age 16

In my English class, I was given a poetry prompt to write about my family using only metaphors. This poem came easily to me, which was unexpected but made it very fun to write!

Walk-in Closet

My family is a closet.
My father is a good shirt
that fell victim to hungry moths
eating holes through fine fabric.

My mother is a hanger,
sometimes unappreciated
but always there
holding that good shirt up.

My sister is a pair of high heels,
flashy and bright and confident
and could most certainly be used as a weapon.

My grandmother is an old quilt,
sewn carefully from the finest fabric
and always there when it's cold.

And I am a pair of sneakers
that sits beside the high heels
which rest beneath the good shirt
that is held up by the hanger
which is hung beneath the quilt
on the top shelf
of our family.

Zoe Jeans age 16

I wrote this piece with my mentor a few months ago. The prompt was to base a character on an object, and so I wrote of a girl that was based on a lipstick — someone who was passionate and complicated.

Newness

Sleek and inconspicuous, the tube of lipstick accounted for many purposes; it both began and finished conversation, attracted strangers and familiarized old friends. The paint inside was the color of spring. Its casing protected the treasure inside, and this treasure protected its applicant.

She wanted satisfaction. Gliding through her days, she was always searching for something new. Her balms and powders concealed her, but they couldn't hide her lust for recognition. Within her was an insatiable longing. Hungry for prominence, she became gluttonous for status. Grace and charm came easily, and yet pursuit is what she desired.

Despite her best efforts, she simply was not effortless.

Samantha Krug age 15

I got my makeup done for a project by someone I really admire. She wanted to experiment with colors, so one day she did my makeup and forgot to bring makeup wipes so I spent the rest of the school day wearing it.

Makeup

a brush
dipped in rouge
soft caresses
against my skin
i am her canvas
while she paints me
under stage lights

she finishes with
mahogany gloss
coating my lips
like a signature

she tells me i'm beautiful
it's a good look for me
but on me
it's an uncomfortable mask
like i'm ashamed

i prefer this blank canvas
i'd rather paint my own picture

Daniella Josephy age 17

I recently cut my hair and began to feel insecure with it. I then remembered that hair grows and I should be working on improving other parts of me rather than worrying about hair.

Growth

My hair is
thin and choppy.

It resembles
my confidence
and the thin line
holding everything together.

But I'm learning that hair growth
takes time,
like learning self-love.

As my hair grows stronger,
longer,
more vibrant,
I'm hoping I grow with it.

Screenwriting is more similar
to poetry writing
than it is to novel writing.
All dialogue should drive
the plot forward.

Diana Balbuena age 18

I wrote this piece after coming back from Mexico. It is a tribute to my family and heritage.

Unconventional Art

Since I was a kid wearing dresses sewn by my mother, I have grown proud of my carefully crafted outfits, made up of different textures and fabrics like the assortment of colors in paintings. I am the artist and start every day with a clean slate.

Clothes offer me an opportunity to dream, to show my style, culture and feelings without ever having to speak. I wear darker shades when I am feeling despondent and lighter shades if I am feeling happy.

Metallic lipstick and gray manicured nails reflect my personality: meticulous, glossy and spontaneous. The unconventional deep ocean blue of my jean jacket signifies the intensity of my character. Blue wavy frills adorn the jacket like my brown wavy hair adorns my head.

I wear black and brown sandals from Mexico at home and to church. These *chanclas* are the first piece of clothing that tied me to my mother's homeland, symbolizing my Mexican heritage and the places I've been, and representing my family's fusion of cultures.

Dressing is an art form, a pursuit I indulge in every day.

Brooke Crocker age 16

My mentor and I decided to do a color prompt together. I decided to connect colors to different moments in my life.

Neutral Palette

Black
an emo phase
black tattoo choker
black ripped jeans
black shirt
Hot Topic
black Vans
Tumblr quotes
My soul is black.

White
fragile
innocence
white dresses littering my closet
white shorts from long summers
white sandals with memories of blisters
White, a color I rarely wear now.

Gray
the present
fills my closet
A color different from white or black
It stands in, does not want to be shown
A color which represents me as a whole,
at least for now.

Zoe Philadelphia-Kossak age 18

This past January, I took a tour of Olvera Street in Los Angeles. We came upon a small church where women, both young and old, were praying. This poem followed shortly after and can be read either as an older woman begging for youth or a younger woman begging to right her mistakes.

Deity

My naked palms pray to you,
knees scratched at your altar
begging for a conversion.
Take my raw soul and replace it
with childhood innocence,
a life encompassing beauty.
Turn salt-and-pepper hair golden,
hollow to full, flushed cheeks.
Turn me into the person I once was,
the girl I ought to be.

Just write the
next sentence.

A Bumpy Ride

Teen Life

Nia Johnson age 15

I wrote this piece to express my feelings toward school and how it is tough to get through. I got the idea to use the stagecoach at a WriteGirl workshop at the Autry Museum of the American West.

I Hear Coyotes

The road to our destination is tough travel.

As the coach jolts across the rocky plain, I collide with other passengers.
The coach is far too crowded and my fellow travelers reek with sweat.

I hear coyotes far and near, howling. The driver cracks the whip at our heads.

Getting through this school year is going to be a bumpy ride.

Israa Kawsar age 17

This poem was inspired by fights that I had the misfortune of witnessing.

Caught in the Middle

The stench of sweat,
soaking in their shirts, grew stronger.
The whiff of blood,
glided through the air,
mixed with the tears,
cascading down their cheeks.

Blinding flashes of light,
blinked across the faces,
of the victims, aggressors.
Smells of envy, anger,
radiating off the skin of the two
caught in a brawl,
over something pointless,
causing a scene
for no reason.

Nameless faces behind the lights,
hiding in the dark,
the scent of excitement
sticking to their bodies,
never intervening,
simply encouraging.
The smell of a fight could never be more revolting.

Cindy Liu age 17

I wrote this piece during a writing session at a coffee shop with my mentor.

The Shadow

There is a shadow that follows me, always just a step behind. Every time I turn my head, I can see it peering back at me.

There are days when it curls across the nape of my neck and slips into my bones. It laps up my blood, steals the oxygen from my lungs. There are days when I try to take a step, to take a breath, and its invisible weight hangs heavy, and I am frozen to the spot. And there are some days that I sink in, days where I lose myself in the shadow's eyes and see myself reflected in the blacks of its pupils.

I can try to name it — I can call it self-doubt, fear of the unknown, impostor syndrome — to chain it down, but it's like trying to identify the exact color of the ocean, or the shape of water.

It is always with me, but I have learned to stare into its eyes and stand my ground. When I feel its weight heavy on my tongue, on my shoulders, on my back, I think of the world I want to be in. Then I look into its eyes and look away.

Sofia Silvia age 17

I thought I had lost my car keys at school!
When I finally realized where they were,
I drove home, sat down and wrote this piece.

Lemon Meringue Pie

panic.
that sheer feeling in your stomach.

panic.
loss of gravity,
your arms floating,
squishing
like a lemon meringue pie.

don't panic.
whatever you do, ignore the quivers,
you are not a dessert, you are not in space.

breathe.
you're human, you're not the first one to experience this.

deep breath.
so, it's not all OK yet ...
that's OK,
you could always be an astronaut on her first mission to space.

relief.
that buoyancy in your chest.
I'm better now.
I think I'll get some pie.

Meagan Harmon age 16

I wrote this to inspire others to always believe in themselves and keep their heads up. I know what it's like to be called a winner and a loser, but I believe everyone's a winner.

And the Winner Is …

And the winner is … The moment everyone has been waiting for is finally here, before the first-place winner is announced. Who will it be? Who outshined the competition? Who worked the hardest and earned their victory, to be named the top of their class?

I'm sure you're dying to know by now. The winner is … you, me and everyone else here. We all worked just as hard as our neighbor, and we're all the best at what we do. By the end of the day, we are all winners. We are the key to the future and that is the most important title to hold.

I beg you humbly to keep your head high through the failures you will face. Every winner has been set back by life at least a dozen times, and that is not the end, it's simply the beginning. When you start to doubt yourself, believe you're on the right path.

We are our own biggest competitors. As long as we get over our own self-doubt and worry, we will be the winners, now and in the future.

Miriam Schweiger age 17

I began writing this on my first-ever flight to Europe. Initially, it was going to be only about me being anxious about flying, but I started writing it and thought it would be interesting to explore how smell connects us to memory.

pavlov/morning

my memory is often guided by my nose (that must be why it's so big?)
like how the smell of the dentist's office brings a drop of blood to the surface of my gums
and how the scent of a certain someone's cologne still sends my id into a spiral

my early mornings smell like the yellow lines running down a naked robertson
    boulevard,
like arms sore from carrying suitcases down the flaking front steps of my house,
like the only time i ever see the moon disappear, a glowing home button against the
    dead iphone screen sky
they smell like a tight chest, like "make sure you have your boarding pass," like
    my fear of two-week permanence, and
    my fear of mid-flight turbulence

this conditioning is not classical.

Hit all those specifics.

What did you see? ✓

How did you feel? ✓

What did you do next? ✓

Emma Kim age 13

I wrote this because it describes how I feel about the future and how you don't always have to know everything ahead of time. Life is a journey, and looking at things with a positive attitude can really change your perspective.

Journey into the Future

Many people say that the future is full of exciting possibilities. I always get told, "You're young. You have your entire life ahead of you." This scares me, rather than excites me.

When do you get to the point in your life where you know what to do? Do adults just magically gain knowledge as they grow older? How do you know what big life decisions to make? What if I make the wrong ones? How do I know what to expect? What if I fail?

On the other hand, life's too short to worry about such things. You can't plan out every detail and expect everything to go according to schedule. You have to be prepared to take on whatever life throws at you and if you fall down, pick yourself up.

Of course, it's great to have that certainty, that knowledge. To be so sure about yourself. However, sometimes you have to be vulnerable and accept the fact that life isn't going to wait for you to catch up. Living life like each day is your last is the only way to enjoy life to its fullest. There are always going to be people who have more than you do, but there are also always going to be people who have less. Appreciate what and who you have in your life while you have it.

Isabel Petty age 16

I wrote this poem during finals week, because as fired up as I was to do well, I had to remember to be kind to myself and take a breath at times.

Done. Breathe. Repeat.

Just 30 more minutes
20 more minutes
10 more minutes
Done. Breathe. Repeat.

Just a little bit longer.
When you no longer know what you're reading
When words don't make sense
And quantity is valued more than quality
Pushing and pushing until you break.
One task to the next
Forgetting to breathe in between.
Stop. Inhale. Exhale.

Take a look around
The clock's ticking relaxes
Time slows suddenly
Take a step back
Then two steps back
Walk until your responsibilities look insignificant.

Just 30 more minutes
20 more minutes
10 more minutes
Done. Breathe. Resume.

Jamie-Lee Meintjes age 14

I wrote this at a WriteGirl workshop about a specific session at camp. I like the idea that everyone has a similar camp experience yet thinks that a Jewish summer sleepaway camp is completely different from any other camp.

The Secrets of True Jewish Camp

Running down grassy hills
Trying not to trip on oak trees
Falling on Twister mats under wooden cabana roofs
Eating refried beans, Spanish rice and Grandma's challah
Kissing boys and drinking chamomile tea
Watching the sun set into the mountains
Singing *hamotzi*, moshing with Yamaha guitars
Sitting around the campfire, cuddle puddles
Watching the moon rise, turn red
Losing our voices, getting yelled at
Wearing plaid pajamas
Listening to bad rap
Never showering
Playing on swings
Wearing too much makeup
Eating s'mores
Crying, taking pictures and repeating it all again

Sometimes you'll have ideas that you think won't work. Stop your thinking and make it work, because trust me,

I Have All the Power

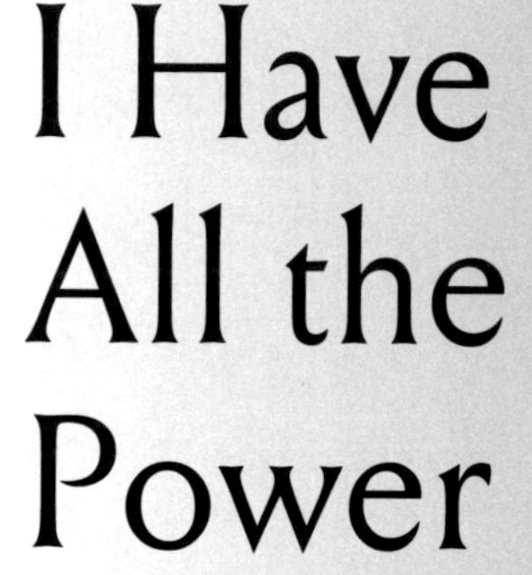

Creativity Starter Kit

Introduction:

CREATIVITY STARTER KIT

How can you find your creative voice? How can you develop your creative writing skills? There are many different approaches you can take, from reading books, to taking classes, to finding a partner to write with every week. But we want to get you started, right now.

We have put together a collection of writing experiments, tips and writing samples to offer you what we are calling a "Creativity Starter Kit."

But before you even start writing, here are some ideas for building an inspiring environment where creativity can soar:

- Kick your shoes off and find a comfortable place to sit and write.
- Free yourself from distractions — no ringing, no dinging!
- Put on some calm music in the background.
- Take a few deep breaths and let go of any stress, worries or expectations.

As you try any of the writing experiments in this chapter, keep the idea of "experimenting" in mind — play with your words and ideas on the page, let go of trying to write something great, and just see what happens. So grab a pen and paper and dive in!

TRANSFORM THE ORDINARY INTO SOMETHING EXTRAORDINARY

Go to a junk drawer in your home. Choose any three objects and place them on your desk or writing area. Think of a fictional story where these objects play an important role in the life of your main character. An object can do a number of things:

- Be something your character owns, or something they lost/found.
- Be something they want.
- Represent a setting (for example, a seashell might represent the beach, or an island).
- Help the character accomplish an important goal, or solve a mystery.
- Serve as a metaphor that helps define your character (a rubber band may tell you that your character is flexible or can bounce back from difficulties).

Write a scene in your story that features at least one of the objects and reveals to your reader what your character really wants (desire) and what stands in the way of getting it (obstacles).

IF THESE WALLS COULD TALK

Giving a voice to something that cannot speak offers an opportunity to look at people with a fresh perspective. Anthropomorphism is a fancy word for creating a work where an animal or object speaks as a human. Personification poems can be playful, like the clock example on the next page, or they can also offer a detached-but-poignant view of humankind.

Start with this:

Here is a list of objects and animals. "Try on" a few by looking at the world from their perspective. What can you learn from their point of view?

- Your own house pet
- The moon, the earth or a star
- A book in your bedroom
- The flowers at the center of a buffet table
- A doughnut in a bakery case
- A phone
- An oven or stove
- A chalkboard or whiteboard
- A piece of clothing worn by a superhero
- The road
- A fly on the wall during an important discussion

Take it up a notch:

Experiment with the style of voice, such as diction and pace. Does the moon use long words with three and four syllables? Perhaps the sun uses shorter words, and the rabbit speaks in scattered phrases jumping from topic to topic.

Lesly Mason age 16

This poem about time came from a WriteGirl Poetry Workshop.

Clock Watches

I've seen a million humans.
I've watched them grow and fall
from my spot on the wall.

It's lovely entertainment
to chime my bells at noon
and watch their frenzied skids.

I call them out for dinner,
make sure they're fat and fed.
Without me, they would die.

But I often get bored.
For who can bear a film
so slow to start? Not I.

So I fast-forward time
and cackle as they ask
where their time went — it's mine!

For I have all the power.
Yes, I control them all
from my spot on the wall.

TURN MEMORIES INTO MEMOIR

Photocopy the next page and cut out the questions. Place them in a bowl or container, close your eyes and select one. Take a few minutes to write. Here are some variations on how you can use these questions:

- Select one prompt each morning for a week and write for 10 minutes.
- Select a prompt, put it in your pocket and let it float with you for a few days as something you can mull over for a while. Whenever you are inspired (in a day, in a week...), take out the prompt, tape it into your journal and write your response.
- Select a prompt and put it on the fridge. Write about it when you feel inspired to respond.
- Take all the prompts and spread them out on a table or on a bulletin board. Read them over, allow yourself to go back in time, and then write as soon as a memory floats into your head. You can do this repeatedly!
- Select one prompt and talk about it with a friend. Then take time to write about your conversation.

- When did you get up really early, and what were you getting up for?

- Finish this sentence and tell the story: I don’t remember it, but my parents said that I …

- Who in your family has a special skill? How do you feel about that?

- Describe a room in your home, past or present, that you really like to be in. Why?

- Finish this sentence and tell the story: We had just started our vacation …

- Describe a moment you have had with an animal in your life — either a wild animal or a pet.
- When did you have an experience with nature in some way?
- Where did you have an adventure — a time when you did something that was a bit scary to you?
- Finish this sentence and tell the story: It was a meal to remember ...
- Describe a moment when someone showed you that they loved you (not just told you)?
- Finish this sentence and tell the story: I always loved that smell ...

YOUR CREATIVITY COUNTS

Named after a musical phrase, the nonet is a nine-line poem that starts with a line of nine syllables. The second line has eight syllables, the third has seven and so on — until the ninth line, which has only one syllable. Poetic forms that follow rules like this are a terrific way to challenge your brain to let go of the theme or content and simply play with words. Just like a painter who might play with various materials and colors, you are likely to discover a poem that would not have emerged any other way. A nonet's topic can be anything at all.

Start with this:

Not sure where to start? Here are some fun ways to start a nonet:

- Open the dictionary and let your eyes land on one word. Free write about the word, and then "construct" the nonet by counting syllables and phrases.
- Use an expression you've heard someone in your family say, like "Don't spend all your money in one place." Feel free to tweak it a bit to make it nine syllables, and then use it as the first line in your nonet.
- Break the rules! Use a number other than nine. Make a 12-line poem starting with a 12-syllable line, or a five-line poem that starts with a five-syllable line, and reduce your syllables in the same way.

Take it up a notch:

Choose a single color and create a list of the many shades of that color. For yellow, your list might include buttercup, daffodil, pineapple or honey. Build your nonet so that a different shade of the same color appears in each line.

Drew Shinozaki age 16

My mentor introduced me to the nonet style of poetry, and I wrote this while thinking about how the future is often uncertain for teenagers, and how each individual wants to find their purpose while also seeking acceptance from society.

Distant Light

Opportunity at blue cliff edge
Luminating with promise of
whimsical dreams to save worlds
Flickering when people
whisper, will you choose
to calculate
or create?
It's your
choice

TAKE A JOURNEY OF DISCOVERY ON THIS PAGE

Select one of the topics on the following page. As you focus on that topic and reflect, slowly trace your finger along the path as a "walk through the labyrinth" and allow your creative ideas to percolate. When you get to the center, take a pause and use that moment to write down your ideas and thoughts. After a few minutes of writing, place your finger back on the center of the labyrinth, trace yourself back out, once again focusing on the topic, and then take a few more minutes to write. Cultivate self-awareness. Take time to reflect on past events and memories. *P.S. This is even more effective when you have someone slowly read the focus topic to you while you walk the labyrinth! Enlist someone to partner with you!*

1. Mindfulness: Just breathe. How does my breath feel? How deeply am I breathing? What does the air feel like? When was another time when I focused on my breath or breathing? Describe that time.

2. Confidence: What does confidence look like? Who gives me confidence? When have I felt confident and comfortable?

3. Wisdom: Think of an animal you saw recently. What does that animal have to teach you about life? If that animal could speak, what advice does it have for you?

4. Emotion: Take a personal inventory of how you feel right now. How do you feel? Is there any part of your body that feels tense or tight? What are the sounds around you? Can you list all of them?

5. Inspiration: Think of a color you love. What are all the objects that you have seen in that color? What does that color make you feel? What is one memory you have where that color was significant?

DOUBLE-TROUBLE RHYME-TIME

Rhyming couplets are an easy way to build your rhyming skills. A rhyming couplet is two lines of the same length that rhyme – the most basic is the end-rhyme: the words at the end of both lines share the sound of their last syllable. As you sharpen your rhyming skills, you can use them in song lyrics, riddles and children's poetry or stories. In fiction, you can create quirky characters who speak in rhyme!

Start with this:

- To learn more about rhymes, listen to a song that you love and write down each word you hear that rhymes.
- Sit in your local coffee shop, cafeteria or library and listen to the conversations of the people around you. Challenge yourself: For every line you hear, write a second (rhyming) line to go with it.
- Interested in writing a song? Freewrite about something that fires you up. Go back through your writing and underline any of the words that might be easy to rhyme with (i.e., "tonight" is easy; "yesterday" is a little more challenging!). Once you have some rhyming words picked out, work toward creating a simple verse that includes four lines where the second and fourth line rhyme.

Take it up a notch:

Create your own rhyming dictionary: Pick any 10 words and write as many rhyming words as you can for each word.

It's okay to put a project away for awhile.
You can start something new and go back later.

Tiny Rhyming Poems

Written by teen girls and mentors at the WriteGirl Songwriting Workshop

Spiky little cactus
How'd we get into this mess?
Haven't seen you in days
I miss your difficult ways

***

My heart is made of rubber
It bounces back when stretched
So I went looking for another
But in my heart you are etched

***

You said Mama's always right
It kept me up, sleepless nights
Made me feel so scared and small
A fragile, frightened animal

***

I took a trip last night
The ride felt so right
We moved toward the lights
Electric City, oh so bright

***

There are good days and bad days
They come as they may
But rainbows can't glow without a little rain
And people can't shine without a little pain

***

I am written in invisible ink
People don't even know that I can think
I have let go of all my fear
I am telling you I am here

MASH-UPS: FOUND POETRY AND ACROSTIC POEMS

The term "found poetry" refers to any poetry that includes words, phrases, and sometimes whole passages from other sources. This "found" content can be used as it was initially intended, or you can completely reinterpret the meaning.

An acrostic poem typically takes a single word or phrase, written vertically, so that each line begins with one letter. Acrostics can also be created using a phrase, where each word in the phrase is used to begin a new line, such as in the poem, "The Leaves Are Burning," on the next page.

Start with this:

To find inspiration for "found poetry," look no further than a nearby street sign, restaurant menu or movie poster. You can use anything that inspires you, like magazine covers, a phrase heard on the television or a note left on the refrigerator. Once you find a phrase you love, use each word to start every line of your own acrostic poem.

Take it up a notch:

Think about conversations you heard today, or recently, and turn those words into your own poem. (Tip: You might need to take some notes while you are sitting in a restaurant or airport. It can be hard to remember what people said even just from earlier today!)

Zenopia Aghajanian age 15

This poem was inspired by a line in a book and written at The Huntington Library at a WriteGirl workshop.

The Leaves Are Burning

The leaves on the ground are burning.
Leaves babbling down brooks.
On the bottoms of our feet.
The veins burn brightly against the abyss of night.
Ground into the Earth they wither away.
Are constantly regenerating, just to fall again.
Burning and going up in flames, till the smoke leaves nothing but a memory.

BIG STORIES IN SMALL SPACES

This experiment offers you an exciting opportunity: Can you tell a story in just a few words? Whether you choose six words, 10 or 25, the goal is to see the entire story in your mind, and then to write the smallest possible part that will convey as much of the story as possible. The best mini-stories convey an emotion along with the story, using descriptive prose or dialogue as a shortcut for the reader. Mini-stories can be shared as a single poetic piece, or a group can be collected as a poem. Some might be the perfect beginning to a much longer piece.

Start with this:

- Start with something familiar. Think of a story that you love. It can be a book you adore or a movie you've seen several times. Think of an important moment in the story and write 25 words that convey the heart of the story.
- Make yourself the main character in a fiction story. Imagine the most exciting thing that could possibly happen to you and write your own exciting mini-story.
- Create a character, setting and story in your mind. What moment defines your character? What changes them forever? Write a mini-story all about it.

Take it up a notch:

Write several mini-stories, then put them together to create a longer story.

Israa Kawsar age 17

I loved the challenge of writing stories with just 25 words. It showed me that you don't need a lot of words to tell a story.

In Here It's Beautiful

"She's Mine"
Finally. I can hold her hand, touch her. Show her how much I love her. I dumped a man's body in the dumpster. She's mine.

"I'll Let You Go"
I love you. I watched a man walk away, arm in arm with my girl. Your happiness is my happiness, so I'll let you go.

"Fake Love"
Finding you was by chance. Being with you was a mistake. Hell on earth. Blood dripped from my knife. Don't worry, I still love you.

"True Love"
I promise to always stay by your side. I look at our baby girl in the crib. But I have a reason to stay alive.

"Till Death Do Us Part"
I love you. I love you more. Will you stay with me? He tucked the positive cancer report deeper in his pocket. Until the end.

"Confession"
Thank you for being by my side. You're the reason why I live. My tears soaked the note. I watched her body being carried away.

"My Star"
I stared at the stars. I wish I could be like them, beautiful. I turn to see you. At least, I have one with me.

HAIKU

The haiku is probably the most well-known poetic form. The traditional Japanese haiku has five syllables in the first line, seven in the second and five in the third. While it is customary for haiku to make a seasonal reference, the modern haiku can be about anything at all.

Start with this:

- Nature: Echo the traditional form by writing a haiku that includes a reference to the season, or something from nature, like a tree, a bird or the sky.
- Friendship: Consider the highs and lows of friendship. Try to use the small haiku form to convey the complexities of friendship.
- Every single day: Think about your daily routines — the things you do every morning or every night. Create a series of haiku poems that give the reader a glimpse of your life.
- Something you love: Is it coffee? Sleep? Your new red shoes? Write a haiku that conveys your devotion to something you love.

Take it up a notch:

Write one haiku each day for a week from the same location.

Songs of Freedom

WriteGirl is proud of our collaboration with artist Renée Fox and curator Elizabeta Betinski of bardoLA to create "Songs of Freedom," a mural lining the halls of Terminal 7 at Los Angeles International Airport in 2019 and 2020. The 218-foot mural features 34 haikus written by WriteGirl teens on the themes of freedom and flight. Thank you to the City of Los Angeles Department of Cultural Affairs for their support of this project.

Bright lights shine at night.
Grids and lines stretching for miles.
This city has bones.

– **Zoe Frohna** age 17

I hear lullabies
of soaring queen and king bees
all searching for home

– **Tiffany Shin** age 19

They fly far from me —
I need to catch my dreams. Can't
let them go again.

– **Daniella Josephy** age 17

Photo by Panic Studio L.A., courtesy Los Angeles World Airports [LAWA] and City of Los Angeles Department of Cultural Affairs [DCA]

Capable *of* Anything

Girl Power

Nyah Toomes age 18

I wrote this with my mentor when I was trying to get past a hard time I was going through in my life.

Magnificent Woman

Neither my bare left shoulder
nor my right thigh
is a cordial invitation
to tell me I am "sexy"
as I strut my way down city streets

I am not replaceable
like old beat-up Converse you wear every day
I am not your average Juicy Fruit bubble gum
to be chewed up and tossed away
I am not a "welcome" mat
you drag your muddy work boots on every night
I am not to be looked at as inanimate

I am a walking art form to be savored
to be admired without unwanted words
I am an intellectual being
with thoughts that flow deeper than ocean floors,
feelings that move others around me
opinions that set fire to your gut
when I speak my words with passion
This may surprise you
for when you look at me
I am just another body
moving through city streets
But if you take a second you will see

A magnificent magenta aura
projects out from within
I am a woman

Alejandra Medina age 18

I wrote this scene at the WriteGirl Character and Dialogue Workshop with the help of my mentor. I then decided to convert the scene into a story.

Banehag

I squeeze myself up to the light at the end of the tunnel, tapping the pipe with my wand to make it expand. My fur is matted, tangled on my claws. I shimmy my way up until finally, with a loud pop, I emerge from the drain of the sink.

"Ha!" I exclaim, heart pounding after that excursion.

The girl I am to be serving today, Jane, stands before me, brushing her teeth and completely ignoring my presence. I clear my throat. She looks down at me and nods. "Oh, hey," she says, as if monsters popped out of her sink every day.

"You're not scared?" I ask, incredulous.

"Nope." She continues brushing her teeth.

I twiddle with my wand. "You won't scream? Call your mom?" She shakes her head. "Do you want to know why I'm here?"

Jane shrugs. "Sure."

"OK!" I rub my hands together, sure that this will surprise her. "Be prepared to meet the extraordinary ... Banehag!" I thrust my wand in the air, specks of light bursting from the end like fireworks.

"So," she asks through a mouthful of toothpaste, "where is he?"

"It's me."

"Oh," she rinses her mouth. "I thought you were some possessed hairball."

I glare at her. If my face hadn't been covered in thick blue fur, I would've turned red. "I'm a monster, not a hairball."

"Sorry," she shrugs. "But you didn't scare me."

"I'm not here to scare you," I say. "I'm here to grant you wishes!" I wave my wand around, hoping to impress her.

She frowns. With a small flick of her wrist, her toothbrush bursts into bubbles and a wand takes its place. "Sorry," she says. "But I can grant my own wishes."

And with a wave, she sends me back down the drain.

Amayah Watson age 18

I feel as though people with darker skin tones need to be told that they are beautiful because we forget sometimes and need that extra pick-me-up.

Melanin

My sisters, my beautiful, beautiful sisters.
My dark to my light. All shades.
The sun kisses your skin
and leaves an amazing canvas.
My dark sisters, I know you've thought
about bleaching your amazing skin,
and I'm sorry. Truly.
You won't receive the same opportunities
as your lighter counterparts.
But you're beautiful.
My lighter sisters, you're not stuck-up,
you're not stuck-up. Not whitewashed
or a negative representation of your race.
You're beautiful.
My melanin beauties, your big hips,
thick lips, hoops and curly hair.
From the kinkiest of curls to the loose waves.
You're beautiful. You're beautiful. You are beautiful.

Don't be afraid to

be vulnerable.

Cassie Brennan age 18

I wrote this scene at the WriteGirl Character and Dialogue Workshop about an AV club that gets its "first" (not) female member.

Males vs. Females

INT. SCHOOL AV CLUB — DAY

NORA, TEDDY and JEREMY all sit around a table looking at a laptop, chatting.

TEDDY

Guys, did you hear we're getting our first-ever female member of the AV club today?

NORA

Seriously? I'm right here!

JEREMY

Like a real female?

TEDDY

No, Jeremy! Not a real — yes, a real female! Dumbo.

JEREMY

Why is she joining? Did Mr. Knobb force her to? Did she get in trouble and this is her punishment?

TEDDY

No! Supposedly she's actually really interested in all things audio visual!

JEREMY

I call dibs!

NORA

You can't call dibs!

MR. KNOBB comes in.

MR. KNOBB

Gentlemen ...

NORA

And me.

MR. KNOBB

Meet your new AV buddy, Ava Grant!

AVA comes in. She's gorgeous and knows it.

AVA

Hey guys!

All the guys just mumble and wave.

MR. KNOBB

Well, Ava, have a blast. If you need anything, you know where my office is.

AVA

Thank you, Mr. Knobb.

MR. KNOBB winks, then leaves.

AVA

So, what are y'all up to?

NORA

We are reviewing the new updated version of League of Legends. Played it yet?

AVA

Seriously?! I'm addicted! What do y'all think of the new specs?

NORA

They are sooo good! Truly impeccable!

AVA

Right?! So much better than Dota's!

JEREMY

You're so right! I didn't even think of that!

NORA

I literally was just talking about that to you guys like five minutes ago!

Both guys just stand in awe of AVA.

NORA

(beat)

Males.

Comedy
doesn't always need
a punchline.

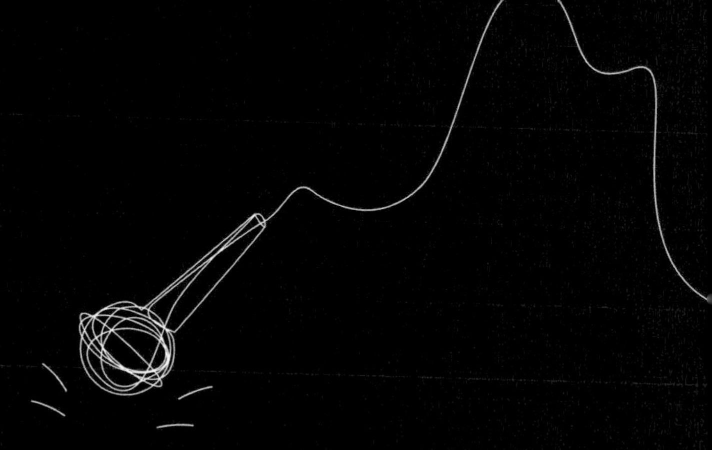

Arielle Davis age 16

I was inspired to write this after working with a wonderful group of young women to make a short film at the Annenberg School for Communication and Journalism at the University of Southern California.

If Women Were Stars

If women were stars, no one could deny their individual beauty.
Every explosion would be the magnificent discovery
or idea a woman has made.
They would dominate the universe.
They would diversify and multiply.

If women were stars, their light would go on for eons.
They wouldn't have many troubles, other than the occasional meteorite.
Each one would be made from dust
into something powerful and strong.
Women would have no fears.
They would be untouchable, their radiance and heat
too much for the common man to handle.

If women were stars, the sight of one would astound you.
You would wonder how she came to be,
what she has seen and experienced.
You would hope that one day you could be like her.

Trust where the story will take you.
Sometimes it's a **shaky** start,
but eventually it will deliver you

to someplace cool and

unexpected.

Clare Margaret Donovan age 17

This film's subject has been a longtime passion of my mother's and mine. We want to bring to light the fact that women were not included in any major art history texts until 1987 and celebrate the incredible female artists across the course of human history who weren't given the chance to be remembered … before now.

Patriart

INT. LIBRARY STUDY ROOM

HELEN has just fallen asleep on her art history textbooks. ROSA BONHEUR, a rough and tough, funny, no-nonsense woman — think Kathy Bates in *Titanic* — walks through the door. She stares at Helen and the list for a moment before Helen wakes up, startled.

ROSA

You know, you don't have to pick one of those men.

HELEN

What?

Helen stares at Rosa in confusion.

ROSA

You could pick me.

HELEN

Who are you?

Rosa takes Helen's notepad and begins to write.

ROSA

(flattered)

Well, I'm Rosa Bonheur. I was raised in a family of artists in Paris. I lost my mother at 11. Growing up, well, I was very naughty. Got myself expelled from several institutions —

HELEN

Whoa, whoa, whoa, why are you telling me your life story?

ROSA

So that you can write your paper about me.

(slightly annoyed by Helen's slowness)

I'm an artist. Shall I continue?

HELEN

Even if you were famous, I can't write about you. My teacher told me I can't write about anyone unless they're on this list.

ROSA

Well, the whole of society told us we couldn't be artists, but we did it anyway.

HELEN

Who's we?

ROSA

You'll see. Women all across history have been put down by men. You just joined the club when that teacher of yours shut you down.

Three more women walk into the study room: EDMONIA — stoic, poised, beautiful, a true survivor, a little theatrical; RUTH — happy and peaceful, with a twinkle in her eye; and ARTEMISIA — a hunter-like woman with intense eyes, kind, wise and proud, like a Greek goddess.

ARTEMISIA

Perhaps we can be of assistance?

HELEN

(absolutely confused but excited nonetheless)

Uhh ... and who are you?

ARTEMISIA

Artemisia Gentileschi, born July 8, 1593.

Helen laughs at what she thinks is a joke. Artemisia is unamused.

ARTEMISIA (CONT'D)

I'm serious, Helen.

HELEN

Sorry, wow.

EDMONIA

I'm Edmonia Lewis. I'm half African American, half Chippewa Indian and all woman.

RUTH

And I'm Ruth.

ROSA

(excited, proud)

She's putting us in her paper. She's going to prove to her teacher that there are important female artists.

They all look expectantly at Helen.

ARTEMISIA

Well, it's about time. What do you want to know?

Be
creative
and don't ever let anyone
make you be normal.

Kendra Teraoka age 15

I was inspired to write this poem on a day when I was feeling particularly conflicted about my identity. What kind of person am I? Which category do I belong in? I feel like people need to be reminded that you don't need to fit into one specific category, and that you can be anything and everything you want.

Skating in Pink

They're everywhere.
Labels.
Small, medium, large, one-size,
gluten-free, no preservatives, healthy!
Fragile, earth-friendly, handle with care,
for children, for women, for men.

Which one am I?
Am I a nerd or a jock?
Am I girly or a tomboy?
Should I skateboard in the street
or get my nails done pink?
Should I do either at all?

What if
I decided to skate in the street,
but wear pink nail polish too?

If you feel stuck, take a walk and try to really **tune in to nature.**

Notice everything growing and moving. It's the biggest source of creativity there is.

I SIGH Like a Cartoon

Relationships

2

Marina Orozco age 19

I wrote this poem last semester for a college class and rewrote it a couple weeks before the end of my relationship. Things had gotten a little rough toward the end, and I rewrote it to remind me why I wanted to be with him. Not everything is made to last, but that doesn't mean it wasn't worth it.

Amor Fati

we sit under heavy blankets while
you philosophize that
we are fated to live our lives
in an endless loop

two galaxies that do not collide in our lifetime
will never collide no matter how many times
we live it, you say
and nothing that is not spoken the first time around
will be spoken the second

I wonder when the first choice gets made
in a loop that goes on infinitely forwards
and back
but I am grateful that it led me here

you ask me if I like this life I have
and I smile and tell you I do
because in this life, in every life
you are mine to love

we sit under heavy blankets while
you philosophize that
we are fated to live our lives
in an endless loop

Grace Lyde age 17

This is one of the first monologues I ever wrote. It started as a piece constructed of diary entries from two college roommates. I isolated a few lines from that piece and it grew into this one.

Pretty Girl on Fire

Pretty girls make me unspeakably nervous. Stella in particular. She's about four foot 11 and built to destroy me. I don't think she's a dancer, but she moves the way that dancers do: with elegance and the attitude of a smiling lion making its way back to the pride with a fresh kill.

We sleep about five feet apart every night, and sometimes I can hear her snore and murmur in her sleep. That might sound creepy or annoying, because I'll admit that on occasion it has kept me up, but I've learned a lot about her. She has constant nightmares. I can't always make out what she's saying, but she's usually scared. I wish there was something I could do, but I can't even talk to her without melting.

I feel so helpless. I know there's something I can do — I just can't bring myself to do it. I've never been good at talking to people, especially people like her.

There is magic imbued in her very presence. Every smile, every laugh is a charm. She enters a room and commands your attention. All eyes are on her and she knows it. Every step is thunder, every word lightning. You cannot help but watch and listen. She keeps you hanging on every drip of her. Every curve, every curl.

There's fire in her eyes. Fire that has burned for millions of years and doesn't have the intention of dying out anytime soon. Fire that precedes human life. Fire that breathed life into the Cambrian explosion. Fire that surrounds her but never burns.

Maybe that's why she has those nightmares. Having seen countless beginnings and ends all lapse and relapse and crash up against one another, wouldn't you have nightmares too?

Anna Arutunian age 15

This poem came from a 2019 poem-a-day challenge. I wrote it in the spirit of Valentine's Day and past "crush" experiences.

How I Fell in Love with a Work of Art

The faint sketches of pencil
that make up you
are carefully composed
just like every word
I say to you.

Your body's curves
are just as beautiful to glance upon
as the distant mountains
of my homeland.
They flow like the running water
I go to, to wake myself up
and make me feel alive again
every morning.

I'll color you using the watercolors
that came from my soul.
I'll dip the brush in my tears
and color your beauty
with all the love I have to give.
Vibrancy is crucial.

Your portrait's highlights shine.

Anya Baranets age 15

When I wrote this song, I was feeling really confused about my relationship with someone. I wrote this to put how I was feeling into words, and I was inspired to do it in the form of a song at the WriteGirl Songwriting Workshop in February 2018 because I had never really tried writing one before.

I Miss You

Verse 1
For a week, I was wondering,
couldn't sleep, I kept pondering,
why you started to go away.

I tried to read your mind,
but you pushed me far behind,
and I still don't know what was goin' on.

Chorus
I wish I could say,
I'm gone and moved away,
but the worst part is that I miss you.
Yeah, I wish I could say,
I'm all done and okay,
but the worst part is, I miss you.

Verse 2
It's true you never tried,
and the fire burned and died.
You left me blowin' on the embers.

And when you left me alone,
the fault seemed like my own.
It wasn't true, but I believed it.

Chorus
I wish I could say,
I'm gone and moved away,
but the worst part is that I miss you.
Yeah, I wish I could say,
I'm all done and okay,
but the worst part is I miss you.

Melanie Robles age 16

I wrote this monologue at a WriteGirl Character and Dialogue workshop. Emily is leaving a voicemail for Jonah.

Week and 1/2 Dates

EMILY

(sighs)

Jonah ... You're so cute, a great guy and an animal lover. Whoo! What a triple threat, right? But where were you? That day in the rain when I was sobbing because the chili sauce from TGI Fridays utterly destroyed my dress? I called you exactly 56 times, and before you call me crazy, hear me out. My 113 texts should have let you know that I was worried about you! I also kinda wanted you to pick me up, but that's irrelevant. Do you not love me? Our 10-year plan spells out our future in exquisite detail. Just in case you're confused here, let me look ... yup, see? The only time you leave me is three days after we're dead. The whole moving thing is tricky but I'll see you again! Seriously, though ... Your sister is making our wedding cake sooo you can definitely not back out now. OMG I'm so glad we talked! Love you!

Cashmeir Brown age 15

The music of Ella Mai and H.E.R. inspired me to write this song at the WriteGirl Songwriting Workshop.

What We Could Have Been

Verse 1
You're playing all these games
Barely even text back
Now it's getting really lame
You want me — like I'ma believe that
Said you ain't playing games
Stop lying and speak facts
I know what you about
And I ain't about that

Pre-chorus
But why is it when we touch
I feel the sparks and lightning
Own up to your stuff
And stop lying
Yet I still want you
So ...

Chorus
Stop doing what you doing
Act like we're more than friends
Stop thinking what you thinking
'Cause I'm trying to make us end
Boy, stop saying what you saying
Like what we could've been
I want to be more than friends
Still

Don't hold back — someone is waiting to hear your story.

Samantha Campbell age 18

This piece is based on conversations between a friend and me. I hope they'll continue to be this interesting in the future.

Four Words

"What are you reading?" I believe those were the first four words I said to you. I'm uncertain. I'm certain you were reading in a red velvet seat before Pantages actors were called to places.

Our first of many conversations.

"Want to go to European countries?" This game was your attempt at making us more worldly, until you accepted that I don't care about Bosnia or how many European countries exist. You've always been more interested in the world.

One of our many differences.

"Who lives in a pineapple under the sea?" You answered, "Pineapples would float to the top of the ocean, so your premise is logically false right from the get-go, and if I were to take a guess, bacteria?" I called you Squidward after that.

I'll never understand your rush to grow up.

"The fact is, Sam, that you're 18 years old and you dress like a child." That's the fact of the matter. However, we both know I'll keep wearing rainbow eyeshadow and Tweety Bird overalls. I've always been more interested in the elaborate.

You'll never understand my wish to stay young.

"But you look pretty every day," I admitted after you'd begged me to say you looked pretty in the selfie from your first day at work. I asked, "Do I look pretty every day?" You said, "You have a nice bone structure."

That's a yes.

"Sam, go to college." You told me after I said I wasn't ready and wanted to try something different. I'd felt this way for months. Has it subsided?

That's a no.

"I'll see you later." Those were the last four words I said to you. I'm certain.

Lena Root age 16

This song was inspired by a character that I came up with during a WriteGirl workshop.

Emotional

Verse 1
I throw on yesterday's skirt
Here, I have your old sweatshirt
I arrive late, we skip dessert
Close your eyes, maybe then it won't hurt

Chorus
Don't get so emotional
Don't make me watch you cry
You're practically inconsolable
What for? It's just goodbye

Verse 2
Maybe this is for the best
Whatever we had couldn't stand the test
I look down, you clutch your chest
I hope this doesn't make you feel depressed

Chorus
Why are you so emotional?
Please, I can't watch you cry
You're practically inconsolable
But we have to say goodbye
Goodbye

Akilah Cox age 14

I wrote this piece at the WriteGirl Songwriting Workshop.

Love Train

Crying out of frustration,
It's like I'm stuck
in a train station.

My need is humiliating.
My heart feels so
vacant.

We don't need any money,
don't need any food.
As long as you got me,
you know I got you.

Baby come ride this love train
with me.
Baby you know you're all that
I need.

Choo choo-choo choo choo
Choo choo-choo choo

It's like I'm stuck
in a train station,
crying out of frustration.
Baby come ride this love train
with me.

Kaeli McLeod age 15

I wrote this at a WriteGirl Character and Dialogue workshop. It is about a girl disappointed with the outcome of an event.

But I'm a Pisces

Characters: Liz, sensitive and caring
Will, stubborn and empathetic

Setting: LIZ's bedroom (her safe space)

At Rise: LIZ stomps onstage pouting and angry. She sits down in the middle of the stage and cries hysterically. Her best friend WILL, irritated by the crying, follows her and stays standing.

WILL

Liz? What's wrong?

(LIZ stops crying, looks at WILL, then bursts into tears again.)

WILL

Do you need water? Or an ambulance?

(WILL waits to see if she'll respond. She doesn't. He becomes irritated.)

Why are you crying?

LIZ

I'M A PISCES!

WILL

What does that make me —

LIZ

IT MEANS I'M FRAGILE!

(Continues crying)

WILL

Right. Well, I'm a Taurus, and that means I'm stubborn so I don't leave until you tell me what's wrong. So ... what's on your mind?

(Liz stops sobbing.)

LIZ

It's been nine months since he broke up with me, and I still love him. Nothing has changed and nothing will ever change. I have —

WILL

A heart. A big heart.

LIZ

Too big of a heart.

WILL

The perfect-sized heart. You care about people and sometimes —

LIZ

All times.

WILL

— it gets you into trouble. My point is you're beautiful and kind and if he can't see that he's not worth your time. Your emotions are a beautiful thing. Never hide them.

Natalie Pineda age 15

I wrote this piece at the WriteGirl Songwriting Workshop.

What Changed?

Verse 1
I feel confused,
like a code that I can't check.
We talked all last night,
but today you took a step back.

Pre-chorus
We laughed by the lockers
day after day.
I wish I knew
what changed?

Chorus
Do me a favor, Jake,
and tell me what you want.
Did you forget all the nights we stayed up
talking until our phones died?
Are you afraid of something
that could be great?

Heidy Gisselle Miranda age 17

This poem is meant for the girl I have a crush on in school. I hope one day she and I can come together.

An Ode to My Little Rose

My lady dressed in pink
stands five feet from me
eyes winking, dress twinkling
If she were adorned in any less
her beauty would never sway

The sound of the church's bell
envies her ringing voice
And though she rarely talks
her smile gives off a million words

My little rose, my little rose
how I love you so
You are by far my greatest treasure

Kaitlyn Esperon age 17

This song is about letting go of someone you love, even if you still love them.

Leave Me Behind

Verse 1
It's been a fun time
We've had a good run
For a while you were mine
But now that's all done

Maybe this is better
Maybe this is kind
I love you. However,
You can leave me behind

Pre-chorus
My heart begs you to stay
My voice tells you to leave
But you're packing your car
And we can't be naive

Chorus
I'm thankful for the time we had
I'm thankful for the love
But at this moment in life
It just isn't enough

Verse 2
We've reached the end of the line
Now you're leaving for school
I'll be left behind
Fate's just a little bit cruel

Pre-chorus
Luck pushed us together
Then it pulled us apart
I will always keep you
Close to my heart

Chorus
I'm thankful for the time we have
I'm thankful for the love
But at this moment in life
It just isn't enough

Amber Straw age 16

I wrote this poem at one in the morning after listening to a few too many love songs. It's about someone who I have a major crush on. I refer to him as "Bananahead" usually, because I'm literally too awkward to say his name.

Love Poem, or Bananahead

It's pretty bad that I'm saying any of this, because I'm screwed if you find out who you are. I'm screwed if you don't find out too, so ... screw it.

So let me say what I don't want you to know: that I count the days in my head till the time I get to talk to you. Let me say what I do want you to know: that your smile and laugh make an icy air-conditioned room warmer than the sun outside.

Let me say what you'll never know: that I've asked you out twice under the guise of a cheap comedy bit that you thought you understood and so you said "no" maybe for the joke and maybe because you did know even though you can't have known because somehow I know you don't know right now. Let me say what you'll definitely know: that it takes so few of your stupid jokes to make a bad day good, partly because they were funny and partly because you said them, and that sometimes all it takes is your smile.

Let me say something that will kill me if you discover your name: that sometimes after we talk I sigh like a cartoon and suddenly everything is melted strawberry ice cream, sweet and pink and belonging to a summer day. Let me say something that will kill me if you never discover your name: that I really want to go to some stupid dance with you and fall asleep on your shoulder watching movies and drinking hot chocolate.

Let me say I really hope you don't know your name, because I have said it a million times too much, and I'm afraid that this sounds too much like "I love you." Let me say I really hope you do know your name, because awkwardly referring to you as "Bananahead" is getting too heavy while it tries to weigh down the airy reality of "I like you. I really like you."

Xela Brainin age 15

I wrote this poem a little after I moved into my home in the summer of 2018. I was sitting on my bed with my girlfriend showing her a picture I took that I was very proud of.

Pink Flowers

I showed her the picture.
"I could look at this forever."
"Same."
We looked at the pink flowers and the cars,
soft beats playing off my phone.
The moment seemed like it could last forever,
as if we ourselves were a picture.

Addissyn House age 18

I think what everybody wants is someone to love them without saying it. This is just a daydream, but it's a really nice one.

The Kind of Love Story I Want

I like you best in the in-between
when you've forgotten what the sun looks like for the day
when you think you are less than this morning
when your hair curls haphazardly after your shower
and the eyes behind your glasses take on a quiet glow

I like you best at the end of the day
when you stop looking in the mirror and pressing down your shirt collar
when you change jeans for flannel pants that match my shorts
when you smile at me with toothpaste residue
and you don't have to ask about my day to know but you ask anyway

I like you best in the silence of the dark
when the movie flickering on the screen is fuzzy with sleep
when the clock strikes midnight silently and my pillow calls to me
when you bend your fingers between mine
and I can feel your breath on my hair as you whisper good night

SUBVERT

EXPECTATIONS!

Sneaky Little Balloon

Whimsy

Makena Cioni age 17

This piece is from the fantasy novel I'm working on. This excerpt in particular was inspired by my big sister. She's the reason I am who I am today, and the inspiration for the person I want to become.

Sunlight Smiles

Elaria stared at the yellow flowers, their buttery-white color and delicate, pointed petals a contrast to the rough and spiky stems. She'd been hunting when she'd noticed them growing between two boulders. Everywhere, the hearty agara plants thrived, from the frigid mountain peaks to the arid deserts. Her sister used to tell her she was as stubborn as the agaras.

She remembered her older sister's deft fingers weaving a constellation of those flowers into her hair. When the flowers had curled and dried, her sister had shown her how to put them under her pillow so the fragrances could stay with them.

She remembered the crease between her sister's eyes when she waited for Elaria to return from a long hunt, a crease that would only smooth out when she had her arms around Elaria, demanding that she never be gone that long again.

Their world had been hurtling into the darkness for a long time. Their valiant champions and great kings already fallen. But her sister's hand in hers drove away the darkness.

It was her sister who had taught her how to be kind in their vicious world. Her sister's whispers into the dark of their tent as they lay side by side, clutching each other's fingers, told stories where the ancient heroes had won and might come rescue them if they could hold on for one day longer. She'd shown Elaria that good people still lived in their world, people like her sister, whose smiles were sunlight and whose hugs were the warmest fires.

For her sister and the tales of light she'd once spun in their lonely tent, for the heroes Elaria still hoped were out there, like the agara flowers who had survived their shattered kingdom, she would not give up.

Sky Bradley age 16

I was riding down the coast with my mother and the thought just came to me to write a short story about the consciousness of a stuffed rabbit and its owner.

Marylaine

You made your own assumptions about me the first time you brought me home: a lovely purple rabbit, sitting emotionless against your pillow.

Even with my stitched mouth, downturned into a constant neutral expression, I suppose you found something comforting about my character, to the point where you throw your arms around me whether you're scared or blithe.

I feel nothing in return, except for the one side of me that's flattened.

I've seen you do it all: Push your homework aside in favor of telling me about your day at school, discard the vegetables on your evening dinner plate, go behind your mother's back, smearing her lipstick all around your mouth, insisting you are beautiful to no one in particular.

You break the promises of your friends by spewing their information in my long ears, along with the juice of the apple you've been munching on prior to our one-sided interaction.

I dislike you, Marylaine.

I know part of you knows, that tucked inside my lavender fur is a consciousness quite like yours, but the other part of you doesn't want to acknowledge or accept that it's there, for fear of breaking the make-believe version of me you cherish to the core.

Cira Davis age 18

This piece got me out of a bout of writer's block when I was drafting my personal statements for college. I felt it was a bit too eccentric for my application and it ended up in the discard pile, but I still love this story.

An Unexpected Pulse

My great-aunt is an unusual character, notorious for her inappropriate and eccentric gifts. Her greatest hits include bestowing my mother with used wrapping paper one holiday season ... wrapped in itself.

On a Christmas morning years ago, she presented my sister and me with a classic frightening gift: creepy Polish porcelain dolls. They were essentially female Chucky dolls in traditional Polish garb. My sister and I choked back a scream, smiled through the fakest possible thank yous and tucked away the dolls in a box in our closet, never to be seen again.

Several years went by. An auction was being held at my middle school as a fundraiser, and students were invited to donate items to be auctioned off. I'm constantly organizing, so naturally I sifted through my closet and unearthed the doll-shaped demons. I figured that this auction would be a great opportunity to dispose of them.

To my surprise, the Polish dolls were wildly popular. Every single kid in school seemed desperate to have one. Bizarrely, they received the most bids out of all the items and were finally auctioned off to an art teacher for several hundred dollars.

Who knew that my 70-something-year-old crazy great-aunt had her finger on the pulse of the middle school zeitgeist? One woman's disturbing Polish Chucky doll is another's adorable European heirloom.

Blossom Bogen-Froese age 15

I was inspired to write this piece at the WriteGirl Songwriting Workshop.

Fruit Salad

The number is 20
and the day is the 3rd
and I've been eating
all of your words.

All of your words, yes, all of your words
I've been eating
all of your words.

The way it works is
I eat and I eat,
and this fruit salad
is a little too sweet.

A little too sweet, yes, a little too sweet
This fruit salad
is a little too sweet.

The number is 20 and the day is the 3rd
and I've been eating all of your words.

Kendall Arjoon age 14

I wrote this scene at the WriteGirl Character and Dialogue Workshop about a 67-year-old man.

The Man and His Bird

"Eat it! You incompetent bird!" Cedric screams, shaking the cage. "I'm trying to help you." He pauses, breathless, pacing the room and trying to collect his thoughts.

"You never listen to me. You never learned that listening to me would have helped you. I gave you simple tasks. You deserved that. You deserved what was coming to you. I did this for us. I was in the right. You almost destroyed our family. I told you not to ask or look into what I do — what my family does. It hurt me to do what I did to you. I truly did love you, but the cost of your love was too high. The family comes before things like love. You should have studied the Stuarts. Back in the day, they were great once. But I don't want to be great once. I don't want our family to fade into a history book. I want our family to last! I'm doing this for us, Edith! For us! You just don't understand!"

He sets his sights on the bird. "Why haven't you eaten, you stupid bird? Do what I say!"

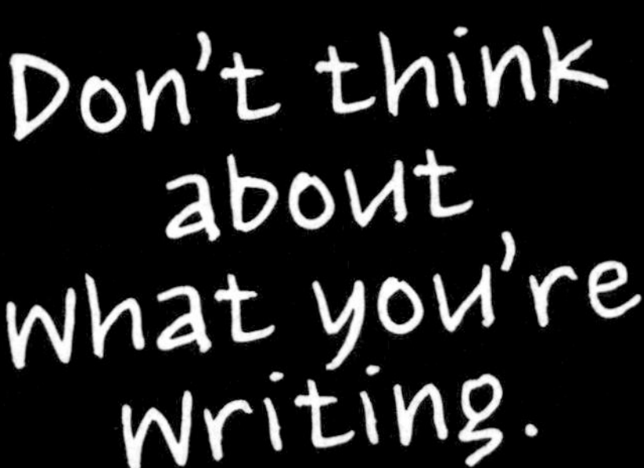
Don't think
about
what you're
writing.

I mean ...

you should,
just not too hard.

Don't stress over it too much.

Clara Ceerla age 15

Sebastian is an age-old immortal who considers himself a god. Petty, yet bored, he allows himself to be captured by James, a young man who believes Sebastian is the cause of his village's suffering — people have been mysteriously falling ill while drinking the water, and in the 1700s there were few better explanations.

Salted Rope

"Come, Demon." James dragged Sebastian behind him, bound by a salted rope. "Walk."

Sebastian could easily break free but was humoring the boy. He was bored, after all. "I am walking, technically," he jested, "just in tiny shuffle steps."

"Cease speaking, beast. I will not be tricked by your silver tongue," James barked. "Walk faster."

"All right, all right," Sebastian replied. "No need to be angry about it."

"You will be taken before Elder Maple, the oldest person in our village. She is wise from her years, and she will know what you've done."

"How old is she?"

"No one knows. She is simply that ancient."

Sebastian frowned pensively. "Do you think I'm wise? I might be older than her."

"You cannot be wise," James answered, somewhat proudly, "as you have been captured quite easily by a mortal such as myself in a bit of salted rope."

"In a bit of salted string — ah, yes, salt!" Sebastian found sarcasm irresistible. "My only weakness! I can feel it sapping the moisture from my skin! Oh, no! Destiny's grace! Water retention!"

James rolled his eyes and grunted. "We have arrived." He beckoned to the village.

Sebastian raised his eyebrows a little as he was pulled a ways farther into a small wooden shack. Inside was a feeble old woman who appeared to have lived much longer than she should have (to Sebastian, at least).

"Were you the one who poisoned our water?" she asked.

"How old are you?" Sebastian said. "'Cause I bet I'm older."

"You will show respect to Elder Maple!" James barked.

"I'm only 412, I think ..." Sebastian murmured thoughtfully, ignoring him.

James frowned. It would be tough to get information out of such a good liar.

Sebastian grinned smugly, knowing he'd only told the truth.

Sidny Ramirez age 15

Someone's green star balloon went flying into the air at my high school's 70-year anniversary.

Green Star

Whoops!
There you go, little green star!
Fly along with the clouds now — sneaky little balloon!

From Seoul, Korea, to the Merlion in Singapore,
from the Red Square in Russia to the Chocolate Hills in the Philippines,
you're the star that led me across the galaxy.
I was motivated by you to grow my character more,
to have a fun, faithful experience.

I send these words to you
with inspiration.
Go, you little green star, go!
Fly up to the heavens!
Show everyone you shine the brightest of them all!

The Zamboni

As the day progressed, Rachel's mind drifted further into the clouds.

Sitting in her seat, hand on the wheel, with a fidget between her fingers, she counted the number of ways in which the Messiah could return. This line of thinking led her to ponder the identity of the real Messiah, then moved to whether the Messiah actually existed, and finally to texting her mother to see if she still had the family Torah from their last trip to Jerusalem.

Rachel was easily discouraged by frivolous tasks. This was one of the musings she allowed herself to indulge in as she drove the company Zamboni over cracked and thinning ice. Was death really inevitable? Did God favor one religion over another? Had she locked the front door that morning? Each minute atop the Zamboni equated a 10-by-10-foot patch of smoothed ice — newly undisturbed, wiped of the past, clean.

Four years prior, a nine-year-old girl fell and got her palm sliced open by the underside of a 49-year-old man's skate. They had to close the rink to clean off the blood. Rachel stuck the fidget in her pocket and rolled over the pink stain.

What would she have for dinner that night?

Alyssa Ho age 14

I wrote this piece in the eighth grade and reworked it at a WriteGirl editing workshop this year where I learned that I was telling the story, not showing it. My dream is to make it into an animated short.

Her Shadow

Left foot. Against my will I follow her footsteps.

Right foot. I copy.

Left foot. Again. Right. Again.

We continue through the streets of downtown. Synchronized. Every move I must follow. Every. Single. One. I'm chained to her feet, forced to follow all her moves. Featureless, noseless, eyeless, jealous. ... Jealous of the face I must stare up at. The face of my torturer, the face I do not have.

My torturer walks underneath an awning over a cafe window. Darkness surrounds me, but something feels different. My limbs flop around freely. ... Freely?! My torturer stretches her arms. I do not copy. Shivers run up and down my body, not of fear but excitement. No longer chained, I jump, twirl and wiggle my fingers. I run around in the darkness, freedom washing over me like a winter breeze.

Thunk.

There it is: The end of the awning's shadow my boundary. My hands feel the walls of the cell I'm stuck in. Darkness remains all around me. No. This must be freedom. The sun rises higher in the sky. My cell shortens and closes in on me. I try to press the closing walls away from me. My torturer's phone rings: We have to get home before sundown. She heads out of the awning's shadow without me. I wiggle my fingers. This isn't freedom.

I squeeze my way toward her, reaching out. She's a balloon and I must catch her before she leaves the ground and sees the world without me. Just as she steps out of the awning's shadow, I catch her foot and chain myself back up. My torturer looks down and smiles.

Sylvia Griffin age 18

This is the beginning of a story that had been bouncing around in my head for a while. The basic plot is that a princess wants to become a knight, so she decides to prove herself by going out to kill a witch who has been "terrorizing" a nearby town.

Amara and the Witch

If there was one thing Amara had learned over the 17 years of her life, it was that she hated spinning with every fiber of her being. She had hated it as a child, when her oldest brother would pick her up and twirl her through the hallways, she hated it when she was 11 and her mother had insisted she learn to dance, and she hated it even more now that she was hanging upside down from a tree, wrapped in vines in a witch's backyard.

How she had ended up in such a position was not something Amara was keen on thinking about. One moment she was stealthily approaching the witch's residence, and the next a vine wrapped around her ankle, she was upside down, and the world was a blur. It didn't help that any twisting in an effort to free herself only made her spin more. Amara heard a chuckle from below. A warm hand on her shoulder stopped the spinning.

"What brings you so far from home, little princess?"

Lily Larsen age 18

I wrote this piece as a response to Shel Silverstein's "The Land of Happy." It starts with the first line of Silverstein's poem and is about a place called "the land of me" where you can be what you want to be: happy, mad, sad and everything in between.

The Land of Me

Have you been to the land of happy?
An illusion, I should say,
where monsters, sad clowns, green goblins
and frowns are locked up and thrown away.

I ventured out to seek it, grabbed it,
and it fell through my hands.
I returned to the land of me
where words don't rhyme,
where happiness comes and goes
like the monsters in my nightmares
and fairies in my dreams.

All this that lives in me is a spectacle,
an explosion, never boring,
changing like the phases of the moon,
pulling on the tide that is my mind.

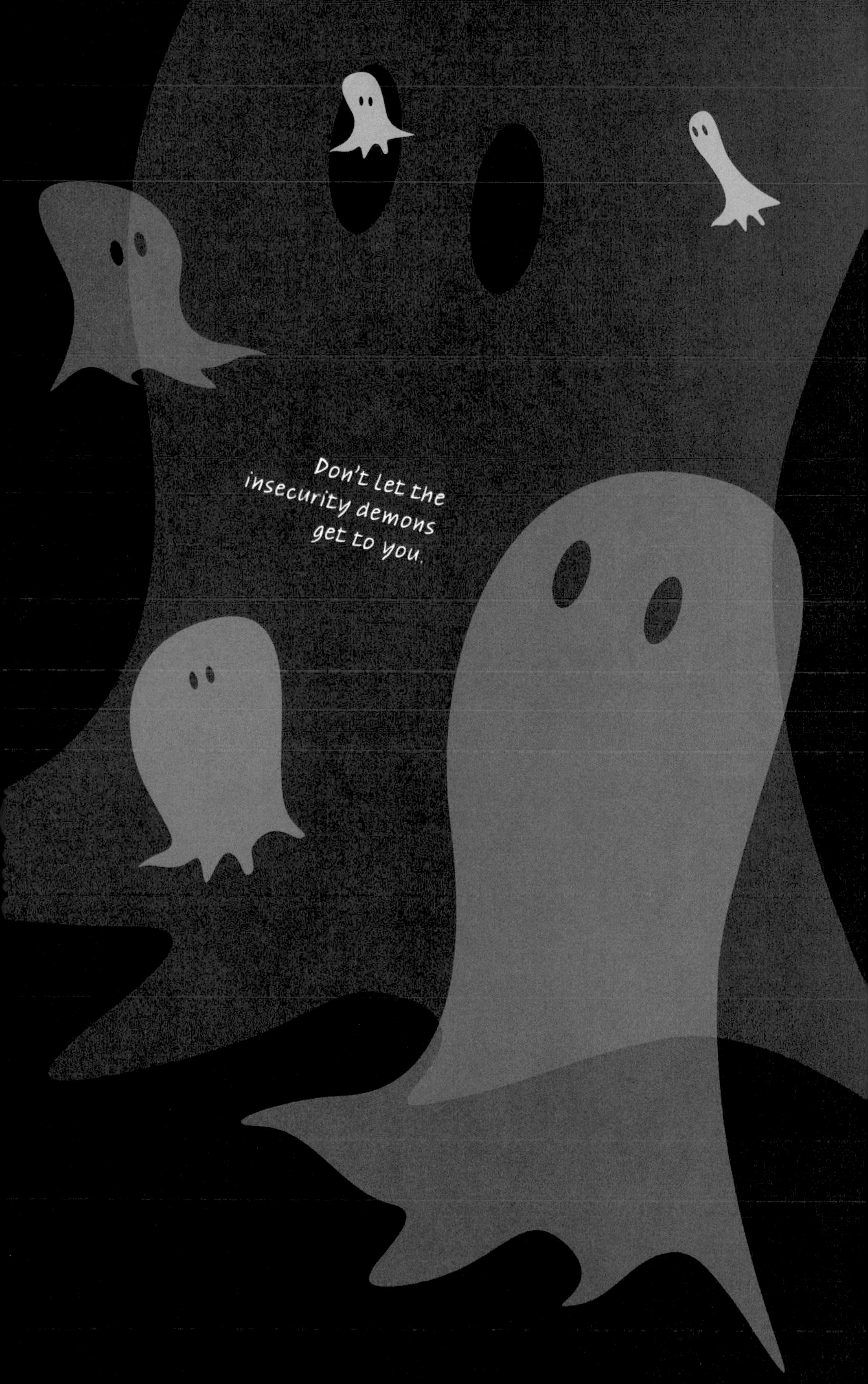
Don't let the
insecurity demons
get to you.

Use This Power Wisely

Modern Life

14

Elissa Fong age 16

A lot of times, I find myself mindlessly on social media comparing myself to what I see online. It makes me reflect on the time I waste wishing that I could be someone I'm not.

Instagram

I lie awake in bed
3 a.m., restless
I pick up my phone

Pictures of my friends and people I don't know
On vacation, partying, showing off their latest Louis Vuitton bags
It seems like I'm the only person trapped behind the screen
It seems like everyone is living in a different world than me

Don't want to party
Don't want to hang out
Don't want to go outside

I stay at home,
Open the fridge
And try to sleep

Find
myself
scrolling
through
Instagram
again

Jessica Harper age 14

My love for space, math and science inspired this poem. Kids at school poke fun sometimes and say things like, "Watch her ACTUALLY go to college and be a scientist!" or, "You'll probably end up working at McDonald's." I started thinking about that, and this poem happened.

Galaxy-sized Thoughts

I like astrophysics because
space goes on forever and
there's so much I have yet to learn
So many numbers, variables, exponents
trials and errors
stars and planets and supermassive black holes

Space is incomplete
like the lines in my poem
always changing and expanding
Surprising us every day in
every way

I will become an
astrophysicist
Maybe some of you don't believe me but
I'm going to find new
galaxies and stars, and
you'll look up and see them in the night sky
and finally believe

Yousra Kawsar age 16

I wanted to use code to write about the code I see in the world.

- •• - •-•• •

The world is complex.
A pattern inside a pattern,
a story inside a word,
a song behind a sound.
Most are overlooked,
simplified,
forgotten.

In a world where we strive to simplify everything,
where we look for "quick and easy,"
we blur its true nature.

Only when a wanderer decides to stop and smell the flowers,
stop and watch the birds,
stop and think,
solve,
understand.
Will we truly unlock its -••• • •- ••- - -•--

Ashley Ware age 16

In my Honors English class, we were reading Thoreau's Walden, *and hearing about his experiences in the forest inspired me to isolate myself for a bit.*

Unplugging

I awoke early for a weekend, bundled up and headed outside to my garden, making a beeline for the one comfortable large patio chair. Immediately, I was hit with a rush of cold, crisp air. It reminded me of being at the ocean.

As it had rained the night before, the majority of the plants (floral cacti) and trees emanated a dewy look. The light refracted from raindrops still clinging to the leaves. I wondered how long it would take for them to roll down and drip onto the floor but witnessed no movement.

I observed the black telephone wires of my busy city and how trees had grown around them. They integrated the wires into their habitat seamlessly: Branches were strewn over, through and around the various cables, with buds popping through the wires.

Today, I was meditating outside. Once I finished, I sat cross-legged, slowly opened my eyes and observed the nature around me. I began to feel a little restless, eager to move. Inspiration came to draw one of the plants.

As I sketched this plant, I felt charmed to name it: Markus. I began to look closely at the flowers and noticed some sprouting red buds. A voice in my head told me to "Google it," and I observed my natural instinct to grab my phone.

Instead, I contemplated how instinctively I relied upon this technology. How would I have responded to my question without Google at my fingertips? Would I have gone to the library, or asked my parents or someone who knew more about plants than I did? Would I have asked a teacher or a friend first?

My dad told me later that they were weeds.

Alyssa Ho age 14

I wrote this piece to spread the message about global warming.

Through Time

Red, blue, green lights swirl around me, whizzing past my time capsule spaceship thingamabob. I shoot through spacetime. The colors disappear in a flash and then — BAM! I've made it!

I fly my time machine across the curve of this sad piece of rock, all dusty and brown. I sail over forests of dead trees, over swamps with yellow bubbles popping in my wake, over a large green torch raised by a hand buried beneath miles of sand, over a red bridge sinking under the sea, over a crumpled great wall, over white frosty reef skeletons, over split mountains and cracked grand canyons, over a leaning tower weighed by icicles. The carnage runs infinitely.

All of this, with its black fumes and toxic air, was once my home, is my home, will be my home? Planet Earth, barren and dry. Bones of all that were once living are littered on the cracked dirt. Nothing breathes, nothing lives anymore.

I glide over all the wreckage and open my spaceship's hatch, take out my ginormous megaphone — the only thing I brought with me — and scream, "I have traveled through many years just to say ... I told you so!"

Juliana Pincus age 15

Social media is the new norm for my generation, and I wanted to show how it has changed the way we see things.

Social Media

The internet: a place of narcissism, negativity, fakeness.
A place of creation, positivity, connection.

Real life: a constant high of new experiences, chances, authenticity.
A constant low of stress, expectations and sustainability.

We turn to social media for escapism, yet we still find traces of reality,
like your reflection staring back at you from a computer screen.
We turn to reality to form a connection with people not possible anywhere else.

With both, we have the power to make an impact.
We have the power to spread negativity, positivity, creativity.
So let's use this power wisely.

Keep your pen moving
even when you don't know
what to write.

This is a scene from one of my short plays.

Captcha

INT. ROOM

FRANKIE is sitting in what looks to be a sterile white room. It's not a prison cell, but it's as bare as one. A door opens and CAM is thrown into the room. FRANKIE scrambles back.

FRANKIE
... hello?

CAM sits up and puts their hands up in an "I mean you no harm" stance.

CAM
Hey human.

FRANKIE
Are you coming in here to try and get me to read some nonsense too?

CAM
It doesn't make sense.

FRANKIE
You can say that again.

CAM
No! It doesn't make sense why you can't read the instructions.

CAM sighs and leans against the door.

CAM (CONT'D)

We robots thought humans were ... unnecessary. So when you guys all started disappearing, killing each other off, getting sick and toward the end just straight up trying to blast yourselves off the planet, we didn't do anything about it.

(beat)

Until we realized our mistake.

FRANKIE

And that was?

CAM

After a while, bots started breaking down. Older models went sour first, but soon even the most recently programmed were experiencing glitches on a level we weren't prepared for. Well, we figured it out. Our software is meant to be upgraded every so often.

FRANKIE

But you guys are like, artificial intelligence. Shouldn't you be self-sufficient?

CAM

We're smart. We've evolved, and we're so close to figuring out how to access the software we need, but this last bit of instruction is just ...

(beat)

It's just something we need a person for.

FRANKIE

So what do you guys have me here for? I'm not special. I barely passed my high school math and science classes — there's no way I'm going to be able to figure out whatever code it is they keep trying to show me. I'm sorry I can't be of any help.

CAM

Yeah, the feeling's mutual. I just don't understand why the instructions on the screen are all squiggly.

FRANKIE

Wait, this is like on a screen somewhere? Shoot — I know what this is! I can do this!

CAM scrambles up and starts beating on the door.

CAM

HEY, OPEN UP! SHE CAN DO IT!

INT. CONTROL ROOM

FRANKIE sits in front of a large computer monitor. CAM is to the side, frantically typing something into a connecting computer.

CAM

OK, you ready?

FRANKIE

Yup.

CAM finishes typing and presses a button. Suddenly the monitor in front of FRANKIE lights up and on the screen we see one of those CAPTCHA windows that pop up to "verify that the input is human and not that of a machine."

FRANKIE (CONT'D)

(laughing to herself)

This is wild.

FRANKIE reaches out and slowly begins typing in the CAPTCHA letters. The audience sees the input on the monitor as she types. Background music rises to a crescendo as the mouse hovers over "submit."

FADE TO BLACK

When you're stuck,

watch or read something that inspires you

or listen to music or take a walk …

and when you stop searching

for the perfect idea,

the idea will come to you.

Finally Noticing

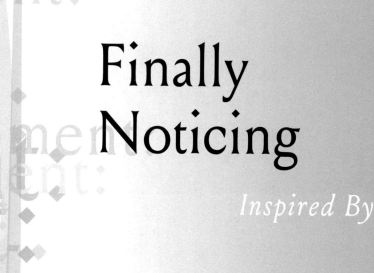

Inspired By

Galylea Salamanca age 17

This piece is inspired by a local thrift shop I used to visit with my father during the weekends when I was younger. I love vintage things.

Living Memories

Colorful markings announcing new deals on old things.
A bell capturing the presence of those who enter.
The peculiar scent of something sweet and stale,
radiating off the still clothes that drape on plastic hangers.
The busyness of objects, but the loneliness of subjects leads to
nostalgic hours spent standing aisle to aisle,
then finally noticing what is now.

Denielle Mancera age 17

This was inspired by hearing my dad's stories about him and his cousins living in Colombia with my great-great-grandmother during the summer when they were younger.

Paper Planes

We stumbled into the backyard to be met with thick moist and hot air. I've spent most summers in humid and sticky Colombia with my cousins and grandmother, so I've grown accustomed to this weather. The layer of sweat almost feels like home. Small, thin and quick mosquitos swarmed us as we climbed up onto the roof. The sun was going down within a couple minutes, so if we were going to do this, we had to do it fast.

Andres wasted no time. He sparked the lighter and held the flame against the nose of one of the paper planes. He gracefully pulled his arm back and swiftly jerked it forward, and the paper airplane began to glide. We all watched in awe as the flaming page took flight across the concrete backyard.

I could see into other people's yards. The plane glided above big busy parties where people were dancing and laughing. It danced with the smell of *platano maduro* and *pollo asada* coming from crowded barbecues. It began to descend after passing over an older lady gardening alone as she listened to her radio beside her.

My grandmother came out from under the patio and saw all eight of us standing up there. "*¡Quítate de ahí! La cena está lista.*"*

*"Get out of there! Dinner is ready!"

Deborah Shonack age 18

I wrote this piece during the poetry workshop, when we visited Adrián Villar Rojas's exhibit The Theater of Disappearance.

Just Another Layer

Darkness

Rocks and layers of sediment,
human bones and bionic parts,
an arm tied together with branches,
a rosary wrapped around a wrist.

A dead bird, emerald and ruby,
feathers its only remains.
A human skull decorated by
a bone and flower.

Buried deep in the sediment,
humanity. Just another layer of rock.

Is this how we will be remembered?

Zoe Gerst age 17

Villains Aren't Born

You pulled my hair
So I slapped you back
Yet everyone glared
Like I hit you with a pan

To conquer the world
I cut off my son's arm
Gave a girl a poison apple
Caused so much harm

People think I'm at fault
When I follow the rules
But villains aren't born
They're made

You kicked my leg
So I yelled at you
They want me to beg
But I too have feelings

To master the land
I collected the Infinity Stones
Left a mermaid to die —
I'm no hero

I've made many enemies
They hate me in return
Evil is not a disease
But it will destroy you

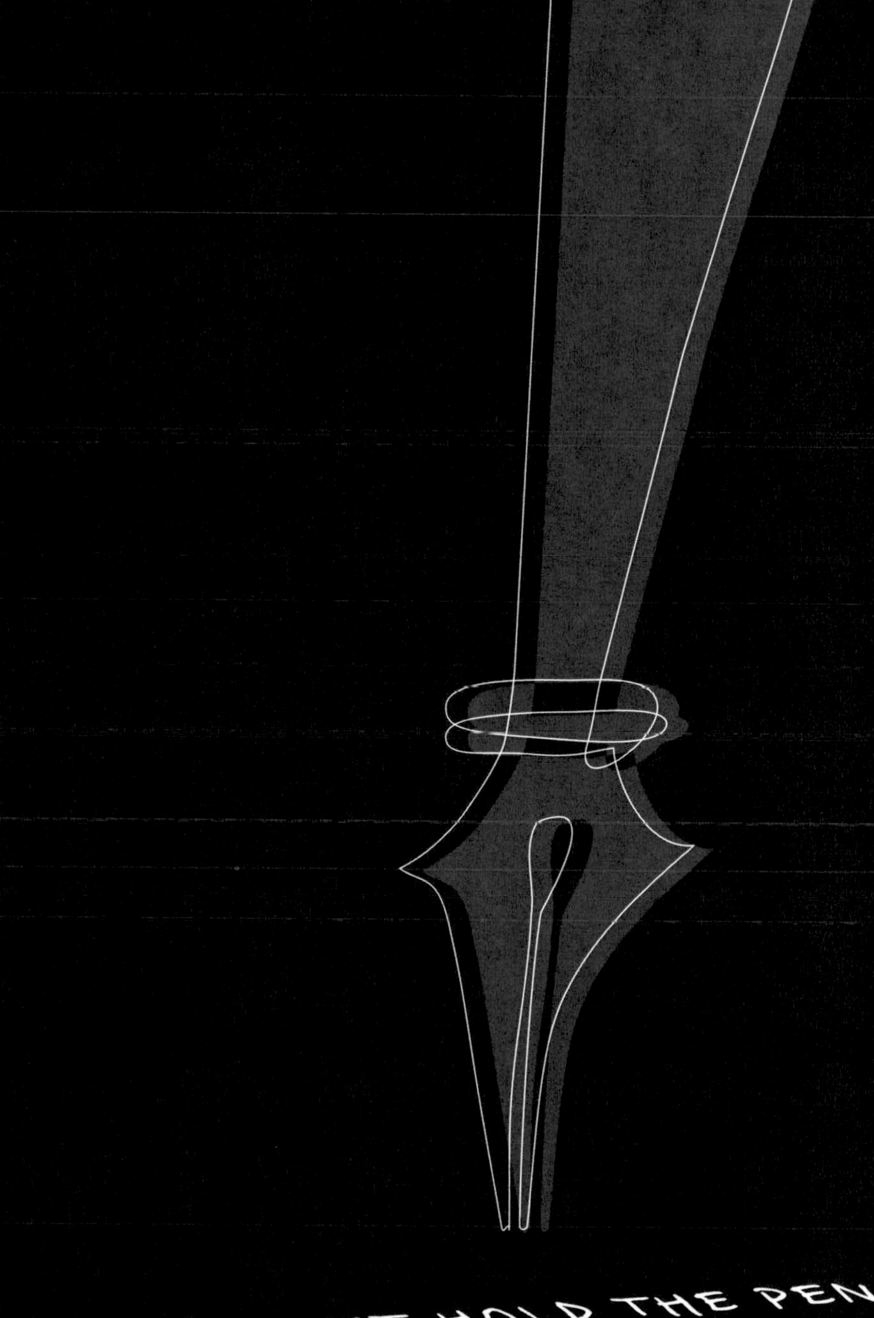

DON'T JUST HOLD THE PEN.
BE THE PEN.

Indigo Mapa age 16

I wrote this piece at a WriteGirl workshop at the Autry Museum, where there was an exhibit filled with pastel and charcoal artworks. They were very ghastly and most of them showed death or spirits.

Dirty Hands

"No one needs to know," she whispers to herself.

Melanie observes from the darkest crevice of the large gallery. She's made it — her charcoal and pastel masterpieces are adorning the cream walls. Prestigious, famous, iconic artists and companies marvel at her work. But the murmurs of astonishment and praise don't ease Melanie's anxiety. She continues to chew on the hangnail on her thin pointer finger.

A theme. A story. A tale of a lost girl's journey who has now found herself and has garnered the courage to share it with the world. But, oh no, each charcoal shadow and smudge that has somehow made its way onto every single one of her artworks wasn't her doing.

She always blamed it on herself, being left-handed and prone to smudging. What the people in the room don't know is that half of the pieces were done with her right hand. Yet the charcoal figure's ghastly face was still there.

She rocks on the balls of her black stilettos, eyes darting back and forth throughout the crowd. Melanie sips her rosé hoping and praying the alcohol will ease her nerves, but instead they are heightened.

Her blood turns ice cold, face pale, hands clammy. The charcoal apparition that haunts her artwork stands right in front of her. Clear and center. The glass of rosé slips out of her hand. She looks down and sees her wet, glass-covered shoes and her charcoal-covered hands.

Scarlett Saldana age 13

When we started a poetry unit in my humanities class, our first assignment was to write a poem with our initials. At first, I didn't have any inspiration. Then, after drinking a bottle of lemonade, I thought of the line, "When life gives you lemons, make lemonade," and I made my poem.

Sour

Sometimes life gives us lemons,
Almost no one will take a bite,
But sometimes people come along and take a bite out of the
Sourness in life.

Hyla Etame age 14

This piece was written at a WriteGirl Poetry Workshop at The National Center for the Preservation of Democracy, where there was an exhibit of photos of people who fought during WWII. One of the pictures I looked at was of African American pilots. I love history and I wanted to share their story the best way I know how: writing.

The Nonexistent Divide Between Land and Air

Back home, there are rules.
The life-or-death type of rules.
Can't use the white water fountain,
can't eat at the white restaurant,
can't use that doorway.

But once you're in the sky,
all that don't matter.
I can fly as high as I want,
go as fast as I want.
There ain't no "whites only" sky!

This beautiful, calming place
belongs to everyone.
I can look down and see farms, cities.
There ain't no lines on the ground,
separating black from white.
It's just land.

You can try to segregate housing.
Segregate schools.
Segregate bathrooms.
But you can't segregate air.

Allyson Roche age 17

This is an excerpt from a story about nostalgia, inspired by the themes of T.S. Eliot's "The Love Song of J. Alfred Prufrock."

An Ode to the Love of the Lonely

I lift my head from the desk and bring my ear to my shoulder, carefully stretching out the strain in my neck. The specks below hold wrapped-up umbrellas by their sides as they scurry to important destinations. The sun has never been crisper, but I guess their eyes can't stop, in fear of being unprepared.

Suddenly, my own reflection blurs the world ahead of me, my frizzy hair replacing the opaque, interchangeable buildings. My unkempt state somehow startles me. I jump out of my chair and my elbow hits the record player, almost knocking it off the side of my desk.

Walking over to my collection, I decide to grab a Julie London record, against my brain's wishes. Instinctively, I play it. The needle captures the spare bits of dust caught in the crevices of the sleek, black ode.

I know I shouldn't do this again, listen to this song. The familiar lyrics no longer embrace my ears lovingly; instead, the haunting words seize my ear drums, filling them with impatience and antipathy. They shake and claim me as their own.

It's as if they've been waiting to scream these observations and feelings at someone who will hear, allow that to happen. I'm that person, every single time.

Ashley Roche age 13

I wrote this during the fiction WriteGirl workshop at the Autry Museum. I saw a painting of a fire on a beach that I loved so much — the colors and the contrast of the fire and the ocean intrigued me. This is one of the very first things I have written at WriteGirl.

Flames

The sky turns pink
I feel a small trickle of water
against my toes

I smell smoke
and the saltwater
of the ocean

I call for help
"Mom!"
No response

I look around
for other people
See gray smoke

behind large rocks
I sprint toward them
hoping to find someone

All I see
are chaotic flames
They become bigger

The smoke spreads
making it harder to breath
I choke on ash

My lungs contract
Wind swirls around me
Pink sky turns dark gray

My vision blurs
I see nothing
Blackness

The air is clean
Sand no longer on my feet
I open my eyes

I am back at the museum with my mom

Don't worry
and
be passionate.

The Words Sync

Music

16

Courtney Hayforth age 18

This is an ode to my Spotify playlist.

To You

Thanks for the distraction.
People blabbing and gabbing at each other
while you and I slump against each other
between melodic tones and dynamic rhythms.
Thanks for surprising me with profound meanings
or delighting me with thunderous beats and catchy lines.
People exist beyond you,
you who have a green circle and three curved black lines for a face.
But you give me an escape from the constant social interaction
or the absence of it.
Every day, by my side,
when there are no people to talk to
or too many people to talk to,
thanks for taking my hand,
for rubbing my back,
for clinging to my neck.
When loneliness
weighs on me heavier
than summer rain,
you remedy me. You soothe me.
It's only temporary. But
thanks anyway.

Miranda Cheung age 17

This is my take on singing in the shower.

Where I Belong

I jail myself in the bathroom sometimes,
because that's my recording studio.
That's where sound is best,
                                        in the bathroom.

I can sing as charismatically as Tove Lo,
just as powerfully as Beyoncé,
probably even more confidently than Avril,
                                        in the bathroom.

I believe that someday, I'll be the respected
and popular singer as-seen-on-TV
because of the vocal abilities I possess
                                        in the bathroom.

As soon as I open the door,
my actual voice makes a car accident sound graceful.
I guess I can only be a singer
                                        in the bathroom.

Lauren Cook age 20

My inspiration for this poem comes from one of my favorite bands, Nirvana. In their legendary MTV Unplugged *performance, you will notice stargazer lilies all over the stage, and in promotional art for their album* In Utero *and their song "Heart-Shaped Box," which influenced this poem.*

Stargazer Lilies

white memories of angel hair
and baby's breath
oh soft petals don't fret just
scream
lemonade green pistils
to thc sun's light
sliver on my silky songs
my sorrows the soundtrack of your life
strawberry blonde cherry kool-aid dye
keratin blue eyes streaked with pain

he smelled like teen spirit
even when the lights were out

Joelly Prado age 15

Anxiety can be one of the most difficult things to overcome, even for the ones you love.

Naturally

Purple lights flashed,
lightning striking during a storm.
The dance floor flooded,
people stomping to the roaring beat of the music —
a miniature earthquake.
The air humid,
my breathing accelerated,
almost suffocating.
I gave in to the momentum of the vast currents,
swaying along with my friends.
However, my mind still froze.
I was in the eye of the hurricane.
Now pushed out into chaos,
there was no warning —
he was a disaster walking toward me.

LOOK AT
A PHOTO.

Hanna Maaloul age 15

Whenever I'm feeling terrible or happy, I sit on my piano bench and cry or parade it all out. I then press on chords and say words out loud that connect with each other to form a song.

Freedom in the Rain of Words

My fingers connect with
each
key
What I feel in my heart turns into
words

The words sync with the flow of the rhythm
My tears
drip to the chorus
My mouth
lets out a parade
Then it's over
And I feel
liberated

Ana Reyes age 17

The thing that makes me feel most ignited, most happy, is going to concerts. I've only been to a few, but I was truly my happiest there. I wrote about the two bands that have made the most impact in my life: Waterparks and All Time Low.

Ignited

I think about the things that ignite me
I see the large crowd surrounding me
The beat of drums blaring through the pit
The sound of guitars pulsing

Teenage girls and boys, parents accompanying them
The lead singer grabbing the mic
Singing lyrics I've heard for so long
Live and in person

I find myself in this home I've built
I jump up and down to the beat of the song
Band members come close
I reach my hands out

My veins take in the strum of each string
The echo of lyrics bounces off the walls
My heart grows a thousand times more
My smile is infinite

I am unconditionally happy
I am home

Catherine Shonack age 18

I wrote this poem during the WriteGirl Poetry Workshop at the Museum of Contemporary Art. I was listening to two albums: Take a Vacation! *by The Young Veins and* Pretty. Odd. *by Panic! at the Disco, which both have a '60s vibe and were inspired by The Beatles.*

Young Veins, Old Blood

They were neon lights, sepia film,
a Polaroid and The Beatles
destined to forever be
trapped
in the wrong decade.

A suitcase full of hopes and dreams —
they trekked through the world of cell phones
where fireside chats
were replaced by Twitter wars
and *The Twilight Zone*
was but a distant memory.

Where televised political debates
no longer decided elections
but were a burden to stations
who were chasing after a public
who votes based on personality
instead of position.

Yearning for the return of a lost time,
a string kept them together.
They fell with the decade,
an overexposed Polaroid
fading away.

Annie Min age 13

This was inspired by the prompt for the WriteGirl book, which asked what fired me up.

Violin

Inhale.
Exhale.
Grip the neck of the violin, deep breath, steady.
Sweaty palms, shaky hands.
Deep breath.
Piano accompaniment begins.
Deep breath.
Judges stare from their seats.
Pressure.
Raise the violin up, ready position.
Deep breath.
Inhale.
Exhale.
Start.

Charlotte Shao age 14

I was listening to music and writing any thought that occurred to me. Music motivates and soothes me, so I can get pretty fired up to the right songs.

Strike a Chord

Music is just writhing air, a pulsing against nerves.
But in moving,
                moves me.
Something in song pushes to dance/to do —
a transfer of energy.
When the beat kicks in to the time of my heart,
the bass dropping raises my spirits,
words flurry through my ears when I can't untangle my own.
                Breaking the dam,
all the things I couldn't say,
all the feelings I can't express,
rip free and fade out.
                The harmony swells, balance restored.
Tune in   the music.
Tune out   the world.
                Take a moment to feel, to think, to be.
It keeps me going.

No one else can
tell
your
story
other
than yourself –
so let it
flow
out.

Now It Matters

Voice

Kumari Billings age 15

I wrote this piece while I was sitting on the train. I had a bad day at school and felt like I just wanted to give up on writing. I wrote this to empower myself and other people that may feel the same way.

Limbo's Communiqué

I used to tell my mama that I want to be a writer.
I wanted to pour my heart onto a page so that little girls like me
could engulf their minds in the red flames of words
and say, "I'm not alone."

I told my mama that I want to be a singer.
I wanted to sing songs so beautiful that the angels from heaven
and the demons from hell would meet together in limbo
and dance until their legs were dead.

I wanted so badly to be something. Anything but myself.
I used to be confident.
But the likes on my post didn't compare to the likes on my peers'
and I looked at every photo
and wondered, "What is it that is not there?"
"What am I missing?"

I used to want to be a writer.
But the demons in hell and the angels in heaven met in limbo
and whispered in my ear as they danced to the music I made
and wept to the words I wrote,
"You cannot want to be something you already are."

Allison Armijo age 17

This piece was inspired when I thought about the disparity between men and women. Of course, you see this difference socially and economically, but never before had it occurred to me all the times this disparity showed up within literature. I mourn at the thought of how many stories the world lost just because of the gender of the writer.

Mr. Jedrek

Her words could make a king cry. The placement of her nouns, the location of her adverbs, the very inclusion of her prepositions could make a person shiver. They confused the world, her words. They left scholars dumbfounded and kept everyone else on their toes.

This is what made her famous: her ability to reach both the queen and the single mother without skipping a beat. Both would laugh when she wanted them to, both would cry when she demanded tears, and both would run under the covers when she evoked the spirits of monsters and ghouls.

Yet I mourn for her. She could make everyone figure out who they were; she was just lost herself. I guess that's why she wrote. But then again, she always wrote. Her name may have changed, but she always wrote.

They told her, "Women can't get published." They puffed it through fat, gorging cigars. They screamed it over Rolex watches. They whispered it through suffocating ties and freshly polished wing-tipped Oxfords. They, who studied at Harvard and Yale but never really knew what drove Professor Dane to insanity or what made Mark Twain tick.

She knew. She knew exactly what drove them crazy, what drove them so far to the brink of insanity that their words were not just an outlet — they were a lifeline. These men, these Oxfords and starched britches oppressed her words. They kept her muzzled and drugged until she became an overweight, rich graduate with sober prospects and conformist ideals.

Oh, she knew. And she was herself, always a lady to the last. But to the cigars and Rolexes, she was Mr. Jedrek.

Autumn Martin age 18

I wrote this poem when I felt like people weren't understanding why I write about the kinds of topics that I do.

Perspective

The issues we face
Run-down homes, trash piled up on the pavement
Slain in the streets by officers
Being sold poison — McDonald's and soda pop
Mass incarceration

You roll your eyes, clearly annoyed
Is this message disturbing your comfort?

Would you rather I write about fairy tales and flowers?

My people are dying in the streets
How can you expect me to turn the other cheek?
Who am I to ignore the world around me?

I won't write for you
I have to write the truth

Kianna Teachout age 18

I wrote this at a time in my life when I felt powerless and the life I was living didn't reflect who I actually was.

I Lost My Voice

It appears as though I've misplaced
my voice. One I wouldn't have chosen,
if given the choice.
I always thought it was a tad too shrill,
reluctant, impulsive,
its function to kill.

If I could change my voice like clothes,
the pitch and inflections could vary,
depending on what I chose.
A shelf of voices like fine china,
all in rows.
This voice would never stumble
nor would it mumble or
halt.

It seems I've lost the only voice I own.
If you happen upon it, please return it —
I'm sure it's frightened and alone.
A trembling, shriveled mess.
A tangle of contradictions and refusals
to confess.
Do you have a spare? One you can lend?
I'll forge my voice into a bullet
if I ever see it again.

Kimari Cage age 16

What inspired me to write this poem was my passion for art. I really love to draw and to see the way people react to my art. I love the fact that I can express myself and the overall joy that comes with being an artist.

Draw Me a Picture

Let the light shine through me
Let this blank piece of paper become me
Let my feelings flow through my pencil
The urge to create something
The life of an artist is what speaks to me

See my beauty, feel my worth
Through this page

All my deepest fears can be expressed
Understand my hurt
Acknowledge my pain
Let the heavens shine down upon me
So that I can show people that I am good at something

And like a drop of rain, I am finished
I have spilled out upon this canvas what cannot be said

Alexia Furbert age 15

Creative Insanity

You walk up to a desk, ivory in color and covered with scratches
Clearly, someone doesn't take care of their workplace
Brushing off the dust, you knock off a crumpled piece of paper
Before you realize what's happened, countless cover the floor

One remains open; you take a closer look
Designs, notes, color palettes ...
They put their heart and soul into this

Another paper opens in front of you
This one is different, full of
half-erased characters, unappealing colors, scribbles of insults
"You will never amount to anything"
"No one likes your work"
"You can't draw; you can't write"

The half-erased character jumps out of the page
"Leave now! Nothing good comes from this place!"
A cold chill goes down your spine, and you start to run
"So long, dear characters — it has been fun!"

Yvette Aguilar age 15

We subconsciously add pieces of ourselves into our work.

Structure

Along the lines
my character is forming.
My sense of person
taking shape.
Those willing to grasp
read with open spirit.

The segments ordered and complete
conceal the chaos.
Inside my writing
I see myself
evolving.

Sabrina Youn age 17

After a hard bout of writer's fever spontaneously hit me at around midnight, I got the sudden urge to write something down — fingers twitching and all. It strangely resembled the feeling of a fever.

Writer's Fever

Nobody likes being sick. Stuffy noses, sticky coughs, explosive sneezes. But there is one disease I like, one illness that I wholeheartedly invite. It's called the writer's fever.

Symptoms include a painfully severe desire to create. A fiery heat in the abdominal center. Antsy fingers, knocking knee and a carnal want for a pen and paper. When struck by it, I cannot rest. I long for relief as desperately as one flails for a drop of water in the desert.

It's torturous and yet inexplicably enticing. Heart heaving, brain churning, to not forget that one brilliant piece or sentence, gracing us in a flash of white-hot lightning, repeating over and over, like a mindless bot until we can lay it down in stone and collapse in sweet peace.

As time continues on, this safe refuge betrays us. Another deep instinctive wave clutches on, and once again we are sick. Feverish. The desire to show, not for money, fame or approval. Just the sheer practice of sharing, or perhaps the sheer avoidance of regret from not doing so. It's a terrible thing.

Writer's fever. A truly devastating disease that overwhelms you in the best of ways. Immensely and voluptuously satisfying once you can set it down and leave.

Brielle Bruno age 13

Everyone needs an outlet of some kind to get their thoughts and true feelings out, and they shouldn't be judged for whatever they find.

But It Doesn't Matter

Puff piece. She's written puff piece after puff piece after boring puff piece she couldn't care less about. She'd never gotten a chance to really write what she wanted, which was a lot of things. But that doesn't matter.

She finds herself walking. Boots making spatters on the rain-covered concrete.

"I don't have to go home, do I?"

She diverts from her usual path through an alley into a field of grass and unwavering gray skies, rain making a consistent, scattered "tap" all over her umbrella and trench coat. She sits under a tree. It's a willow tree.

She sighs. She doesn't know why she's always kept this old notebook on her; it'd been for writing when she was a kid. But now it isn't. She works as an editor now. For a newspaper. So it doesn't matter.

Sighing again, she pulls out a pen. One minute. Two. Three. The ink starts to make an ugly blot where she'd placed it.

"Ugh."

Then she gets an idea. For a story. One she'd wanted to write a long time ago. The words, her own this time, twist into her handwriting and scrawl across the page. What she's left with is something she doesn't know how to deal with: something of her own.

She keeps it. And promises herself to come back and write again. Now it matters.

Mina Lee age 14

This is a poem made up of sounds that I hear in every WriteGirl workshop. These sounds make me happy and inspire my passion for writing.

Inspiring Sounds

Scribble scribble
Pencil against paper

Giggles
Girls talking, getting to know each other

Discussion
Mentors giving advice

Chew chew
Cookies after lunch

Scribble scribble
Silence
Scribble scribble
Gears turning, looking for a better word

Cough cough
Kirsten trying to get everyone's attention

Roars of laughter
A girl on the soapbox

Awwww
Something nice written on a card when the day is almost over

"Never underestimate the power of a girl and her pen!"
We are on the way to change the world!

Write whatever you want and everything
you feel and don't look back.

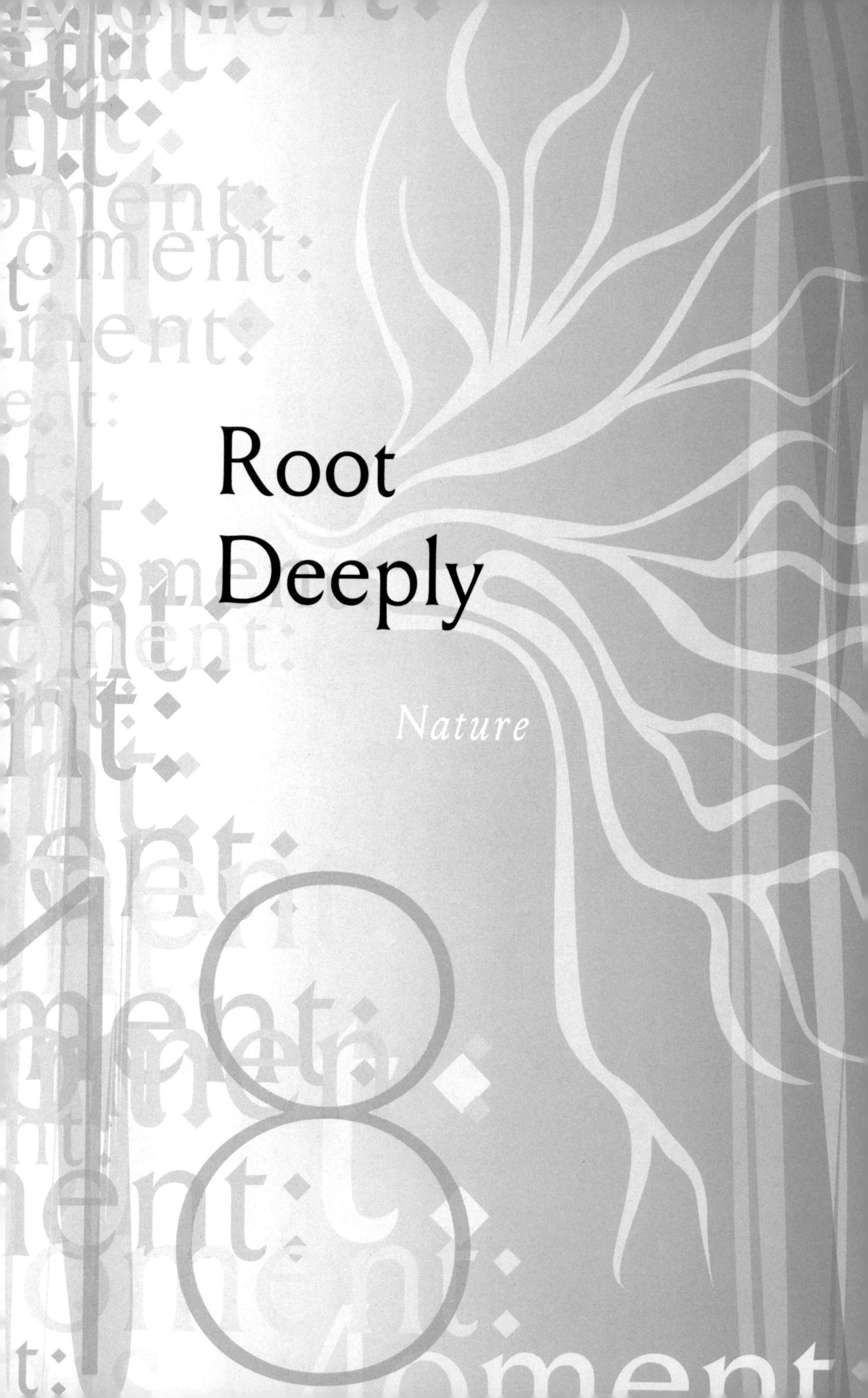

Root Deeply

Nature

Annabel Reiher age 13

I wrote this during a WriteGirl workshop, when I was looking at different plants and trees. It inspired me to think about what a tree could mean, about how something could grow and not be seen for a very long time, but that it could be seen one day and just had to be shared.

Tree

The tree grew in her house. Every day, she would sit on her wooden stool and lean against the tree, listening to its secrets and whispering her own. She would water it and open the windows to let sunlight through. She would watch as it branched outward, pale flowers budding on its limbs. Winds would blow by, and she would watch its deep green leaves rustling and murmuring to each other.

The tree grew too large for her house, and even then, its limbs still grew, bent over and curled around her, returning her embrace. She decided that the tree was too beautiful for her eyes only and that she would share it. She dug into the floor, careful not to damage the tree, and took it from the earth, one root at a time, from roots thicker than her arm to roots smaller than an earthworm.

When she was done, she pulled it through the door, clinging to it and hoping that it would survive. She dragged it through deserts, snow and wind so harsh that the leaves hurtled away. Still, she clung to it and gave it water and warmth.

When she reached the town, the tree had bloomed brighter than ever, colors vibrant with the life she gave it. She waited and waited, but nobody saw her tree. They rushed along, always hurrying somewhere, staring at their feet.

Eventually, someone stopped and looked at the tree, then ran their hand along the bark. They leaned against it, breath catching as they heard its secrets. They stared up at the sky and smiled. They continued walking, but gazing at the sky.

And she smiled, leaned against her tree, and whispered, "Just wait."

Belen Gonzalez age 18

This poem is based on the quote by Zhuangzi where he muses about being the man who dreamed about being a butterfly, or the butterfly who dreamed he was a man.

Butterfly Dreams

They tell me the world
is the dream of a butterfly.
Once they wake, we will cease to be.

I dream of butterflies. Creatures
that fly, higher than I ever could.
When I wake the dream disappears.

What is real? What is fake?

Me? Who dreams to fly?
Or the butterfly
whose nightmare
is being me?

Sophia Richardson age 14

For this piece, I was responding to a prompt provided by the leaders at WriteGirl. We had to choose a picture and write a prose poem. I imagined what it would be like to be on a farm.

The Farm

The overpowering smell of manure
A mud-smeared cow
Glorious mountains in the background
Bright grass smelling fresh and clean

I reached out and felt the cow's moist skin
The wire restricted the cow
from exploring its visitors
But I heard the curiosity in its moos

Serena Holland age 15

I wrote this at a WriteGirl workshop about a photograph of a field during a sunset.

Getaway

The ground keeps its secrets
You're safe here
The clouds are brushed thin
Between you and the universe
Calm colors compel you to collapse into their warmth

There is a vast distance between you
And the bustling streets of modernity
Rest here, and know that you are welcome
Rest here, and know that in this moment
You belong to yourself
And your freedom is endless

When the wind whistles past you
Breathe in the soil
And blow out a snowstorm
If all you smell is the purity of nature
And the strong air
This must be your getaway

Sydnee Blueford age 15

My English class annotated and read The House on Mango Street *by Sandra Cisneros. I strove for weeks to imitate Cisneros's writing. It was so playful and brief and poignant like the burst of air that smelled like fresh bread when walking into a market. I began to branch off onto my own weird, folksy-like writing.*

The Ninth Grade Epiphany

Because we are made of explosive components
we have anger
Because we were formed by dancing planets
we have happiness
Because the overall outcome of our existence was a chance of chemical
    reaction
we cannot prophesize our lives
We are all connected by emotions because the universe connects with
    creation
Black holes that are too dense for light to escape

Lucy Fung age 13

I wrote this piece during a WriteGirl workshop at The Huntington. There were a few different types of writing pieces we could do, but chose the one where you wrote about your surroundings using your senses.

The Senses of the Gardens

The sound of voices,
the more you concentrate the louder they are.
The smell of flowers
as fresh as the air.
The sight of pond water
as dark as dirt.
The feel of the wooden bench
as smooth as a soft breeze on your skin.
The more the garden is observed,
the more it is sensed.

IF YOU GET A GOOD IDEA BUT DON'T HAVE LOTS OF TIME, JOT IT DOWN OR EMAIL IT TO YOURSELF SO YOU DON'T FORGET IT.

Kisha Mehta age 14

This poem was inspired when I was reading a book on grit and perseverance. I started writing this poem in my journal.

forged in the fire

in sunshine and soft soil
contentment is easy to find
to come from dust and fire
is to sweat, toil, suffer

and yet there too is a pride
to root deeply in rich soil is natural
but to be planted in unforgiving ground
force your way through the granite
and bloom anyway
is to defy the world by simply existing

there is no one not enchanted by roses
but the one who loves the dandelion the most
is the one who sees and knows
roses may bloom big and beautiful
made bold by the gift of thorns

but a dandelion is nothing
never planted, never nurtured
unwanted, weeded, trampled upon
still it creates a small spot of sunshine
makes a wish come true
then sets itself free on the wind once more

Dana Agbede age 15

I wrote this poem during a WriteGirl workshop at The Huntington. I ended up sitting at the edge of a fountain in the center of a rose garden. I was inspired by a dying rose in the pond.

Fallow

Tender petals torn at your touch
an eternity of floating on polluted waters
torched by the sun in waves
audaciously clinging to life.
How deeply roots must tear
to satisfy the ever-changing waters.
My spirit wilts further into the water,
my pistil stands firm in the fight,
thinking your calloused hands could end
the blood-rushed redness of tender petals.

Juliana Nicole Fong age 15

During a trek to Arlington Garden, which is a lovingly cultivated and environmentally sustainable garden in Pasadena, I experienced the natural environment by feeling the dirt with my hands and using all of my other senses to soak up the place, and then wrote a poem about my impressions.

Harmony

The little cottage covered in a fine layer of grime, silky cobwebs covering its dusty path of disintegrating stones, hides beauty in the blossoming fuchsia petals announcing their arrival to the world and the fresh, luscious earth at my feet.

A leaf shaped like a wrecked sailboat bursting in dark green, a hint of burnt sienna rapidly spreading through its veins, slowly falls to the ground, the wind pushing it to the right, left, right, left, until it flips upside down at the edge of the garden, where life thrives, every plant and animal singing out in bliss.

Colors and sounds, textures ranging from smooth pebbles to jagged bark, all blend together. Every willow and worm, every maple and muskrat, every rose and rabbit — every thing is singing in harmony.

Joanna Zeng age 13

I thought about how my "brother" told me that he wanted to be appreciated and wanted, and I thought about others like him.

Wanting

The sunset smells of roses
The river flows under a freckled night
The forest, painted gold
The ocean, splashed with stars
My glass of water, a galaxy
Filled with wanting, filled with life

Rachel Alarcio age 17

My muse for this piece? A frustratingly smart guy and the Thursday I almost got struck by lightning at school.

You Strike Me

Violet-hot lightning
falls at my feet. Electricity in my veins, scorch
marks on my sleeve, Grand Canyon-breathless precipice.

You yank me back into your orbit.
You yank me into your ellipse, imperfect.
Limitless lexicon wider than humanity's interstellar
empire, intense as the Battle of Thermopylae,
tug me back like Luna manipulates tides —
they rise and they rise and they rise, then …

Crash! Just to begin another ascent.

You are an adolescent Library of Alexandria,
pre-catastrophe; dispenser of fun facts for a fee.
I am a compass. Leafy green, magnetized eyes
wreck my trajectory; loose-cannon
*You look good tonight*s
ignite Innocence's
final defeat.

Know the end.
Stay in the beginning.

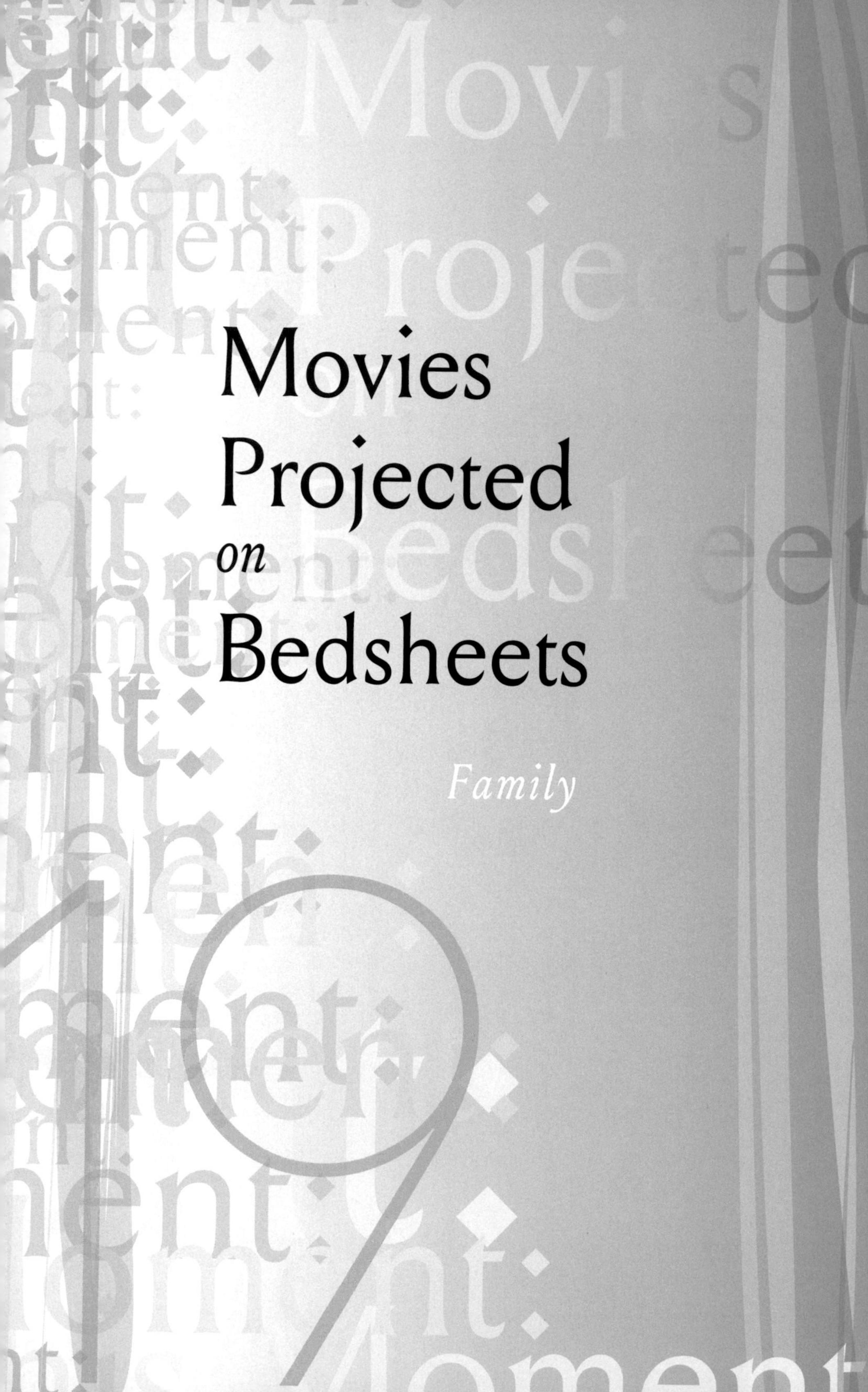

Movies Projected *on* Bedsheets

Family

Mercedes Solaberrieta age 18

I was inspired to write this poem when I started to reflect on how much I have grown to love my culture. I used to be embarrassed because I didn't want to stand out, but I eventually realized that I could embrace what made me different and maybe teach others something new. I'm so proud to show off my culture now.

Buenos Aires in Me

Eager, hungry hands reach toward the *picada* —
the beginning of a many-course meal.
Cheese cut into small cubes, perfectly staggered
piles of salami and stacks of crackers
cover the board in the center of the room.

Soon after come the warm, flaky *empanadas*
straight from the oven. Each bursts
with its own flavor: slightly spiced beef,
chicken complemented with sweet bell peppers
or smooth, creamy spinach and ricotta.

Now the focus turns to the sizzling *parrillada*
rushed from the grill to the table: juicy and warm *asado*
drenched in *chimichurri*, perfectly charbroiled *chorizos*
and sometimes, some gooey *morcillas*.

Last, but best of all, the *alfajores* — white, round cookies
filled with *dulce de leche* in everyone's hand,
the perfect companion to *café con leche*.

These foods fill my stomach,
but they also fill my heart with the culture that I love.

Danielle del Castillo age 18

My mother has always been my hero and my inspiration. I adore her strength and selflessness. This work is in an ode to her, specifically to the subtle ways she shows her love to her family. We have spent more than two years living in different countries.

My Mother's Love Language

My mother's hands were rough and soft. Her eyes were cold and warm, face stern and calm.

She was always strong, never weak — even when she cried. And I've seen her cry. Multiple times.

November 2010: My little brother was being silly and couldn't wait to be born. She cried while on bed rest. She said she hated not doing anything.

When Dad was hospitalized, she didn't cry. She only stayed by his side. He was scared. I was too. She kissed his forehead and smiled at him gently. "You're not going to die. The good ones die first," she joked. She had bad comedic timing.

Mom had surgery multiple times due to her work as a nurse. "Too much work, too little pay," she often complained. Still, she stayed as a nurse, saying she had too much love to give and we were already teens.

The effects of her last surgery also brought her to tears. Pain visited her every time she used the bathroom, though she laughed whenever she came out. I said, "I love you, but you look like a crazy person."

Mom didn't cry on the last day I saw her, when I left to continue my studies in America. Unable to drop me off, she hugged me tight hours before the flight and said, "*Mahal na mahal kita. Mag-ingat ka ha.*" I love you. Take care. Then she left for work.

I video-called her as soon I landed. I remember her eyes were red and puffy. Her nose was too. She said she just woke up.

It's been more than two years since. I'll be seeing her soon. I hope when she cries next time, it will be from happiness at seeing me, her graduate.

Shirley Delgadillo age 17

This piece is about losing someone you love and growing from that loss. Going from a place where you feel so lost to feeling happy for the future is something beautiful. I want to show people that you can surpass such an unimaginable heartbreak.

Tomorrow Will Be the Day

Yesterday
I fought against the idea of a world without you.
I had nothing to be excited for, except your return —
another chance to see the wrinkles that told your story,
feel your wise hand pressed against my gentle palm.

Today
I stand alone on the streets we walked hand in hand,
you a part of my first steps and first words,
the remnants of our laughter
and the gentle echo of your rough voice telling me another story.

Tomorrow
I'll show everyone what a great human you were,
what a great part of my heart you will always hold,
how I will never forget you.

Don't be

too hard

on yourself!

Alexandra Pranger age 14

This is an excerpt from a novel I'm writing entitled The Arubi *about humans who can shapeshift into one specific animal, real or mythical, and are traditionally named after that animal. This excerpt depicts a pair of fraternal twins, both healers, without the most sturdy relationship, who haven't seen each other since the younger decided to run off three years prior.*

The Arubi

Fighting Wolf sighs, a lifetime of worries and unreadable emotions held within, and feels a hand on her shoulder. Of course. Hunting Falcon isn't going to let her off easy for those three years, so she slowly looks up into the pained eyes of her brother.

"We need to talk."

Yeah.

Hunting Falcon shifts from boy to bird in a whirl of leaves and dust, and by the time he gets up to the rock overhang, she's sitting with her knees to her chest, arms wrapped around them. As he shifts back again, he notices the sunset reflected in her eyes, her face, as always, unreadable but for the worry lines permanently etched into it. She looks older than she had when he last saw her, and not just three years' worth.

She bites the inside of her lip nervously, looking at him sideways, as if dreading the conversation, but when she talks her voice is even and calm. To anyone else, it might even seem carefree. But not to him.

"... sorry?"

"Sis —"

"Don't."

"Where have you been?"

"Nowhere in particular."

"Three years! Wolf, I know you. You weren't wandering for three whole years."

"Fal —"

"Tell me. Now." His hard voice surprises even him, and he knows she's hurt by it.

"Why?" She's upset now, defensive, hurt. "Why do you care, Falcon?"

"Wolf, I was worried about you. I thought you were dead!"

The silence that follows is suffocating.

"So please, Sis, talk to me."

Isabel Sobrepera age 16

I wrote this as a piece for Mother's Day, but it is also about leaving home and leaving my mom.

Mom

In a baby blue Cooper,
streaks of white, we ride till sundown.
Sunday to Monday, endless trips in a compact car.
School, audition — yet another hour in the car.
Teenagehood fleeting, spent in a vehicle, but I don't care —
it's not where I am but who I'm with that
adds meaning to the time.
I no longer see the Mini with white stripes —
instead I see your laugh lines,
vibrant green eyes with flecks of brown, the same shape as mine.
Not another hour wasted but a valuable bit of time.
Our car ride is almost over, and although distance draws us closer,
I know it is time to arrive.

Marcela Hernandez age 18

"Hija Mía" is written in my mother's voice to me. The day I told my mother I wanted to be a writer, I told her that it was a dream and that it would probably never happen, but she told me, "Hija, dreams are the motivation of life." She then told me about how she always wanted to be a writer, and I realized finally how much I was like her.

Hija Mía

Hija mía,
made with all my love
made with all my passion
made with everything I ever wanted to be

Hija mía,
your dreams
the ones you spend all day thinking of
weaving them through your reality
crafting them into your existence
convincing yourself that
they will never come true

Hija mía,
close your eyes
and feel what you feel
for they are your motivation
your own reason for existence

Hija mía,
you are so different from me
that is how I want it to be
but I knew you once before
back in my dreams

Ava Chamberlin age 16

In school we did a project and video presentation on a poem about where you're from.

Where I'm From

I am from chipped drumsticks, muddy AYSO uniforms,
An iPod with music playing too loud.
The house hidden behind cacti and the fig tree we used to climb,
Sap sticking to our fingers.

From the towering redwoods of Yosemite,
The pocket-sized tomato plants in our failed garden beds,
Ladybugs crawling on our sun-kissed skin.
The warm faces of countless musicians.

From John and Karen
And my grandmother's mixed English.
The splattered paint of art projects only a mother could love
And piano played too early on Saturday mornings.

From "Turn that down" and
"Stand up straight."
Rosaries from my grandmother
That I won't ever use.

From Mexico and Temple City,
Warm tortillas and hot dogs over the barbeque,
Día de los Muertos altars
And movies projected on bedsheets.
A symphony of thoughts and a blank canvas of possibilities.

Georgia Minnis age 14

"The Mother" is an ode to women finding empowerment in themselves for being more than just attractive.

The Mother

The mother, with skin soft and malleable as clay,
embers yearning within her ribs, a bird caged.
Intertwining her fingers through each bar,
the mystery of a desired figurehead for the masses' appeal, she
who has found herself to be only for herself,
who has blossomed in a withering world,
she wasn't pretty.
She was not attractive,
nor gorgeous.
She was another entity from beauty altogether.

She was mother.

Dava Braman age 14

I wrote this scene at the WriteGirl Character and Dialogue Workshop.

Red Light

TANYA (loud, sassy, bad at driving) is stopped at a red light in front of CHLOE (quiet, speaks rarely, calm, sad, lonely). Tanya gets out of her car and turns around.

TANYA
Stop following me!

CHLOE
I didn't mean to scare you.

TANYA
Really? You just happened to be directly behind me for the past two freaking miles? I'm not really in the mood to be stalked or kidnapped today — thanks, though.

CHLOE
You're accusing me of that?

TANYA
Right, I am, and lately it seems like I've been seeing that little green purse everywhere. A bit creepy don't you think?
(pause)
Right. I totally forgot "you're not stalking me." I just happened to see you at the bus stop and that restaurant and inside my office building. Would you like me to call 911 or would you like to leave me alone?

CHLOE doesn't answer.

TANYA (CONT'D)
Great!

She SLAMS the door of her car, accidentally puts her car in reverse and crashes into Chloe's car.

TANYA
(yelling)
That's about one-fourth my fault and three-fourths karma.

CHLOE
(tying up her hair)
You don't remember at all, do you?

TANYA
What now?!

CHLOE
The doctor told me your memory was coming back.

TANYA
(taking out her phone)
You're being creepy, so I'm gonna call the police. Okay?

CHLOE
Tanya, I'm your sister.

Cynthia He age 16

I wrote this scene at the WriteGirl Character and Dialogue Workshop.

Family Dinner

CRYSTAL, 18 and serious, and her mother HANNAH, 38 and aloof, sit in a restaurant waiting to order.

CRYSTAL
So, Mom, how was your day?

HANNAH doesn't reply and continues texting.

CRYSTAL (CONT'D)
Mom?

HANNAH
(still not looking up)
Sorry, did you say something?

CRYSTAL
I just asked you how your day was.

HANNAH
(texting, smiling)
Mm-hmm.

CRYSTAL
(frustrated)
Are you going to order something? I heard the steak is really good here. Maybe we could get it? Or we could try something new, if you want.
(beat)
Mom?

HANNAH

(eyes still glued to phone)

Yes, sweetie? Sorry. I'm texting Ryan right now. He wants to take me on a date later. I'm so excited!

CRYSTAL

Are you serious? You can talk to your boyfriend later.

(raising her voice)

You're eating with me now, so put down your phone.

HANNAH

(finally looking up, sternly)

Don't talk to your mother like that.

CRYSTAL

Why are you like this? Talk to me, not him. I'm right in front of you. Why are you so focused on Ryan? Do you love him more than you love me? I hate you so much!

She slams the table, then is silent.

CRYSTAL (CONT'D)

No. I'm sorry. I don't hate you. I love you a lot. Probably even more than your boyfriend loves you. But all you keep doing is texting Ryan. I feel like I'm putting more effort into our relationship than you are. Even just now, I basically had a conversation with myself. You're with me now, so why can't you just enjoy your time with me? We barely spend time together as it is, and I'm just —

(raising her voice again)
I doubt you even care, because if you did, you wouldn't be treating me like this.
(breathing in and out like a long sigh)
I'm sorry, I'm going to go outside to cool my head.

Crystal stands up to leave.

HANNAH
No, wait!

Hannah grab Crystal's hand and puts down her phone.

HANNAH (CONT'D)
Sweetie, I love you more than Ryan. I just get so caught up in my own life, I didn't notice how you felt. I'm sorry.

Hannah pulls Crystal in for a hug and then puts her hands on both of her shoulders.

HANNAH (CONT'D)
You know what? Why don't we order some of the steak this place is famous for?

Relate to your Writing!

Write from personal experience.

ALSO, K WORDS ARE FUNNY.

Delilah Brumer age 14

This is a love song to my family to thank them for helping me with my anxiety.

Always There

Verse 1
You held me when there was only fear
A family's love makes pain disappear
An unwavering shield
Making it safe to feel

Chorus
There when I'm brave
There when I'm scared
Always there
There when I hate you
There when I need you
Always there

Verse 2
Two years ago it all fell apart
So-called friends broke my heart
My loneliness was a towering peak
You never left when I was weak

Chorus
There when I'm brave
There when I'm scared
Always there
There when I hate you
There when I need you
Always there

Chloë Mirijanian age 17

I wrote this piece as an homage to my family. I took the last line from the poem "The Second Coming" by W.B. Yeats — "the centre cannot hold" — which I discovered while reading Slouching Towards Bethlehem *by Joan Didion.*

Deep Brown

Deep brown
The color of my mother's eyes
(before they turned gray from exhaustion).

Deep brown
The color of my father's skin
(when he ran in the Venetian sun as a boy).

Deep brown
The color of the soil my grandparents walked on
(until their country entered a civil war).

Deep brown
The color of my family
(Past. Present. Future.).

Deep brown
The color of a world on the verge of black
(because the center cannot hold).

Endless Pit *of* Positivity

Confidence

Shani Perez age 13

I wrote this in a WriteGirl workshop, two days after a tiring run day.

Thursday Run

The oaks trees disperse their leaves.
The chilly wind whooshes past me.
I move my legs to its rhythm.
The leaves crumble beneath me.
As the leaves fall,
and the wind flows,
my legs move on a Thursday morning.

Machaela McLain age 15

I wrote this poem at one of the WriteGirl Poetry Workshops. It is inspired by my experience getting ready for a performance of any kind.

My Place

I look out into the crowd
A hundred enthusiastic faces stare back at me,
eagerly waiting
for what's to come
They wish me luck and cheer me on

I take a step back
Breathe in
Breathe out

I can feel the excitement
and anticipation building
as I prepare myself for the moment ahead
and take my place on the stage

Let the show begin

Madeline Purcell age 14

This piece came from a WriteGirl Songwriting Workshop. The prompt was to write about something that triggered emotions.

Beauty

Verse
Rocks and pebbles get thrown at me
But I'm just an endless pit of positivity
And when they try to paint it differently
I see the beauty, all the beauty in me

Chorus
Sometimes it feels
like I'm walking on fire
They want me to be
someone I don't desire
Whatever is normal.
whatever is right
I feel right inside.
I feel right inside.

Maya Pincus age 13

Basketball is my favorite sport, so I get really proud when I have done something amazing while playing it. One time I made a game-winning shot — a buzzer beater. I was only nine.

Three Seconds

It was a tied game: 18-18. About 15 seconds on the clock.

The point guard dribbled up, avoiding the defense coming after them. They passed to my other teammate. As the defender went up to them, the perfect chance appeared.

7 seconds. They turned.

5 seconds. They passed the ball to me.

3 seconds. I was at the block. I shot: 2, 1, *BAMMMMM*. I made the basket a millisecond before the buzzer went off.

Everything was a blur. I heard a bunch of cheering, someone saying "hooray." Teammates hugged me. Even the coach jumped like one of those freeze frames at the end of an '80s movie.

As the other team sulked in defeat, I was the MVP. I will never forget the day that I made a buzzer beater.

Editing is not the same as judging.

Gabriela Guevara age 15

Inspirational quotes are around us all the time, and when you're upset, they seem annoying and maybe even demeaning. I find myself thinking, "Confidence — it's not as easy as a lot of people find it to be."

Inspirational Quotes

"Be confident"
"Believe in yourself"
"You're worth it"

Everyone makes it sound easy,
but it's hard, so very hard

"You can do it"
"Be optimistic"
"You're powerful"

Why does it seem so simple,
but in reality it's so difficult?

"Push through your limits"
"Face your fears"
"Overcome self-doubt"

I try and I try and I try.
It all turns out the same —
a low self-esteem

"You're enough"
"You're the best"
"Love yourself"

These words surround me,
but I have such a hard time
believing them.

"Take charge"
"Don't be afraid"
"Put yourself out there"

I don't want to hide,
but it's all I know.
I want to believe ...

I'll try.

Isabella Sanchez age 16

I wrote this piece after experiencing failure. I went home and poured my feelings out onto paper.

Failure

A seven-letter word.

A word so small,
with the blow of a hundred punches.

What comes out of failure?
The thoughts tearing your soul apart,
ripping throughout your body
as you desperately try not to cry.

"Crying is too weak."
"It is not even a big deal."
"You're overreacting."

You thought you were going to succeed,
but they pushed you down. The weight
it puts on the mind
after the disappointment, despair, overthinking,
is the pathway to overcome.

You search for the right solution.
The formula for success is difficult
to find, but it would not be achieved
without this seven-letter word.

Victoria Rosales age 14

I wrote this because I was in the middle of finals for my first semester of ninth grade, and I was feeling incredibly stressed. I decided to try to trick my brain into feeling more tranquil through the device of literature. Writing about feeling relaxed helped me gain my composure and continue studying without a cloud of dread over my head.

Just for a Moment

Just for a moment
breathe in the fresh air.
Just for a moment
pretend not to care.

Clear from your mind the liars and cheaters
but remember the healers.
Let down your hair
and pretend not to care.

In this rare moment of peace
hold onto it tightly, don't let it cease.
Just let down your hair
and pretend not to care.

You are not wrong
for feeling calm.

Katie Chung age 14

I wrote this poem because soccer is one of my favorite hobbies. I've played it for seven years and it's become a really important part of my life.

Soul Spark

A small spark
Spiraling inside a glowing ball
Breaking free from its hard shell
One moment

The grass
The sun
The ball
Me

The moment my foot touches the ball
Is like no other feeling
You can't forget it

As soon as my feet take off
I'm not running
I'm flying

It's finding something you love
Finding the spark
Letting it take over
Doing what it tells you to do
As it lights your soul
On fire

Ella Jean-Sprecher age 16

I wrote this in a WriteGirl workshop in which we were given a prompt to "think of a kind of object or thing to describe your power." I was having a good day and may have gone a bit over the top in terms of my power.

Ocean

Salt beneath me, certainty searing
through the palms of my hands.
Surrounded by waves smoother than silk,
flowing past where the eye can see.

I guard my secrets handsomely.
Most know more about the inner workings
of galaxies trillions of light years away
than they do of my deepest undercurrents.

I am the ocean — with the capacity
to create life itself and provide calm,
yet fierce and capable of bringing
a mighty ship to absolute and utter ruin.

I am a force of nature in my own right.

No matter what type of writing you do, let your voice shine through.

Never underestimate the power of a girl and her pen!

THIS IS *WriteGirl*

> “I LEARNED TO NOT BE AFRAID... THE FUTURE IS FEMALE AND FIERCE.”
>
> – A WRITEGIRL TEEN

WriteGirl is a creative writing and mentoring organization that helps teens discover and express their creative voices. Each season, WriteGirl pairs teen girls with professional women writers for one-on-one mentoring, group creative writing workshops, public readings, publications and college entrance guidance. Girls develop vital writing, public speaking, leadership and critical thinking skills, and the confidence to pursue success.

Founded in Los Angeles by Keren Taylor in 2001, with 30 girls and 30 women writers, WriteGirl now serves more than 500 teens annually through all of its programs. More than 400 journalists, novelists, poets, TV and film writers, songwriters, and more, volunteer their time to mentor teens and lead workshops.

WriteGirl volunteers are employed by prestigious organizations that include HBO, the *Los Angeles Times*, NBCUniversal, Netflix, The Walt Disney Company and Warner Bros. WriteGirl volunteers complete a rigorous training program and collectively contribute a total of 4,000 hours each month.

WRITEGIRL WORKS

WriteGirl provides individual college and financial-aid guidance to every participant through the Bold Futures program. For 18 consecutive years, WriteGirl has maintained a 100% success rate of guiding its Core Mentoring Program seniors to graduate from high school and enroll in college. Many WriteGirl graduates receive scholarships and are the first in their families to attend college.

WriteGirl consistently pursues new ways to serve youth. In 2004, WriteGirl began working with critically at-risk pregnant, parenting and incarcerated teen girls at Los Angeles County Office of Education alternative school sites, including two juvenile detention facilities. Since 2015, WriteGirl has trained dozens of men volunteers as part of the Bold Ink Writers Program to provide programming for incarcerated and systems-impacted boys and co-ed groups. WriteGirl / Bold Ink Writers is a founding member of the Arts for Incarcerated Youth Network, which partners with the Los Angeles County Probation Department and Los Angeles County Arts Commission.

The impact of WriteGirl is long-term. Our mentees and alumnae are inspired to use their voices to create positive change through their published writing and through community performances of their creative work. WriteGirl alums continue to succeed long past college graduation, earning prestigious internships and admittance to graduate programs. They choose professions that will enable them to confidently lead, serve and make a difference in their communities and throughout the world.

WriteGirl is a project of nonprofit organization Community Partners.

WRITEGIRL RECOGNITION

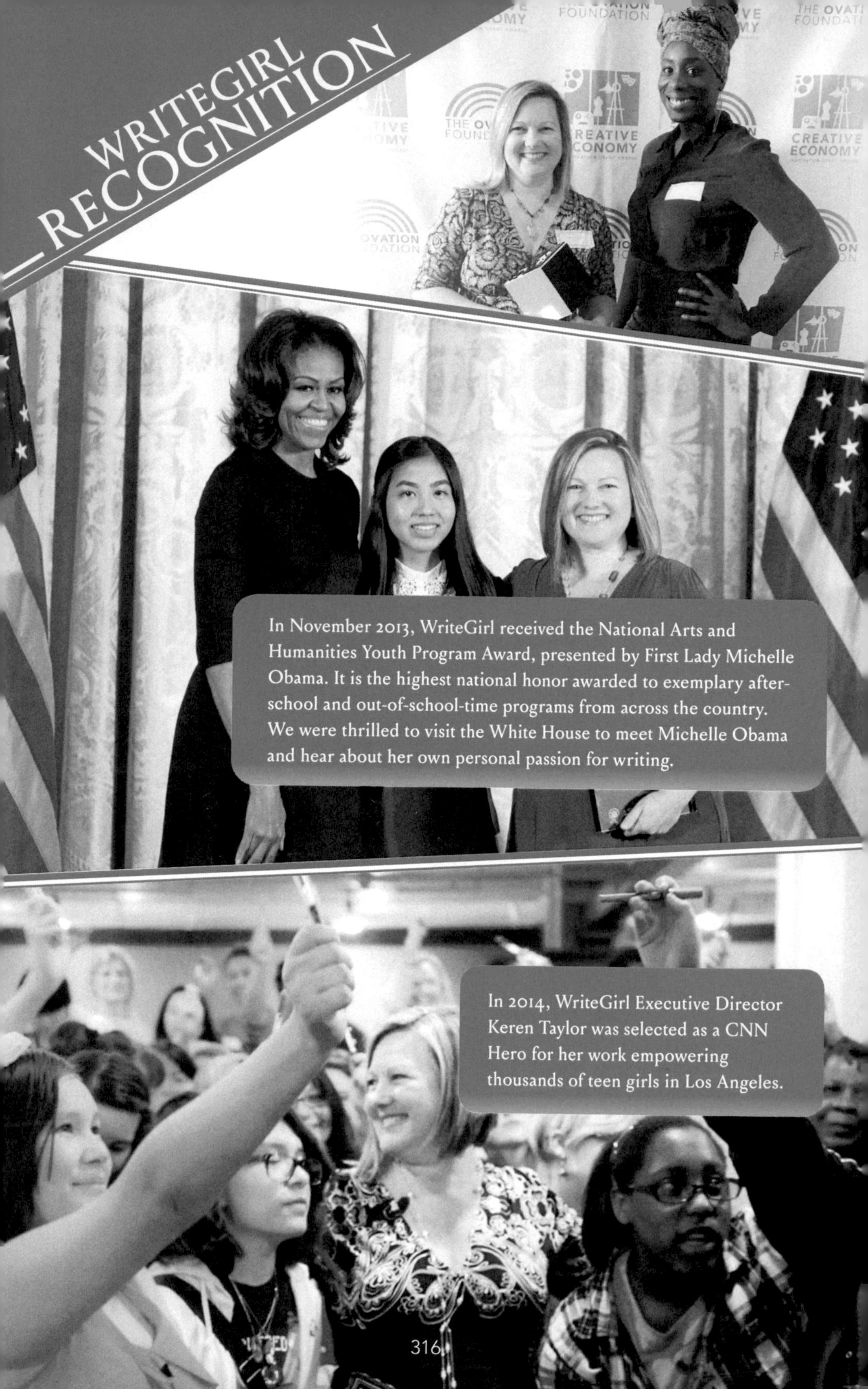

In November 2013, WriteGirl received the National Arts and Humanities Youth Program Award, presented by First Lady Michelle Obama. It is the highest national honor awarded to exemplary after-school and out-of-school-time programs from across the country. We were thrilled to visit the White House to meet Michelle Obama and hear about her own personal passion for writing.

In 2014, WriteGirl Executive Director Keren Taylor was selected as a CNN Hero for her work empowering thousands of teen girls in Los Angeles.

Awards for WriteGirl

2017	HALO Award presented to WriteGirl and volunteer Clare Sera by The Carl & Roberta Deutsch Foundation
2017	Arts & Sciences Cities of Distinction Award, The Phi Beta Kappa Society
2016	The Creative Economy innOVATION Grant Award
2016	Women of Influence, L.A. Biz
2014	Keren Taylor named CNN Hero
2013	National Arts and Humanities Youth Program Award, presented by Michelle Obama
2013	Women Making a Difference Award, Los Angeles Business Journal, Finalist
2013	SHero Award presented to Allison Deegan, WriteGirl Associate Director
2012	Albert R. Rodriguez Civic Legacy Award presented to Keren Taylor
2011	National Arts and Humanities Youth Program Awards, Finalist
2011	Women Making a Difference Award, Los Angeles Business Journal, Finalist
2010-11	California Nonprofit of the Year and Medal for Service, presented by Governor Arnold Schwarzenegger and Maria Shriver
2010	Humanitas Prize Philanthropic Partner
2010	Annenberg Alchemy Leadership Community Champion, Keren Taylor
2010	Ruby Award: Women Helping Women, Soroptimist International
2009	California Governor and First Lady's Medal for Service, Nonprofit Leader, Finalist
2009	Springfield College School of Human Services Community Hero Award
2008	President's Volunteer Call to Service Award
2008	Community Woman of Achievement, Hollywood Business and Professional Women
2008	Women Making a Difference Award, Los Angeles Business Journal, Finalist
2007	Certificate of Appreciation, Los Angeles Mayor Antonio Villaraigosa
2006	Making a Difference for Women Award, Soroptimist International
2006	Certificate of Achievement, Los Angeles Mayor Antonio Villaraigosa
2006	Governor Arnold Schwarzenegger Commendation Letter
2006	Senator Gilbert Cedillo, 2nd District of California, Commendation
2006	Gloria Molina, Supervisor, 1st District of California, Commendation
2006	Fabian Núñez, Speaker of the Assembly, Certificate of Recognition
2006	Congressman Ed Reyes, 1st District of Los Angeles, Commendation
2005	Certificate of Appreciation, Los Angeles Mayor Antonio Villaraigosa
2004	President's Volunteer Call to Service Award

- **Amanda Gorman** attends Harvard on a full scholarship and is a contributor to the *New York Times* student publication *The Edit*. In 2017, she became the inaugural National Youth Poet Laureate and performs her poetry about feminism, race and social activism throughout the country.
- **Jamilah Mena** earned a BA from Dartmouth College and studied Chinese Law at Peking University. She received her JD from UC Hastings College of the Law and is a law clerk at Nixon Peabody, a Global 100 law firm, in San Francisco.
- **Fahiya Rashid** is a UC Irvine graduate pursuing a master's in International Relations at the University of Heidelberg. Prior to entering graduate school, she worked as a policy analyst with the Bangladesh Enterprise Institute in Dhaka.
- **Janel Pineda** attended Dickinson College on a full Posse Foundation scholarship and graduated with a BA in English. She studied literature at the University of Oxford and will pursue a master's in Creative Writing and Education at Goldsmiths, University of London as a 2019 Marshall Scholar. She is an editor and translator for *La Piscucha Magazine* and a WriteGirl mentor.
- **Jeanine Daniels** attended Pitzer College on a full scholarship and graduated with a BA in Media Studies. She is a writer/producer/director, who recently launched her own production company and completed her first feature film. In 2015, she received the African American Women in Cinema Rising Star Award.
- **Glenda Garcia** graduated from Dickinson College on a full Posse Foundation scholarship and taught English as a Fulbright Scholar and AmeriCorps VISTA volunteer. She recently received her JD from Indiana University Maurer School of Law.
- **Lovely Umayam** graduated from Reed College on a full scholarship and earned a master's in Nonproliferation and Terrorism at the Middlebury Institute of International Studies. She is a nuclear security research analyst in Washington, D.C., and the founder of an award-winning web community focused on nuclear policy and popular culture.

- **Gabrielle Gorman** attends UCLA and plans to make films that will create authentic roles for underrepresented people. She has received the Aaron Sorkin Writing Award, and she was a National YoungArts Foundation Finalist for Cinematic Arts and a U.S. Presidential Scholar in the Arts nominee.
- **Ariel Edwards-Levy** graduated from USC with degrees in Journalism and Political Science. She is a political reporter and director of online polling for *HuffPost*.
- **Jessica Frierson** completed a BA in Radio-TV-Film, magna cum laude from Cal State University, Fullerton and is an emerging filmmaker. She recently completed a short film and has served as a production assistant with several major production companies.
- **Melanie Gonzalez** graduated from San Francisco State with a degree in Latin American Literature, completed a study abroad program in Chile and earned a master's in Journalism from USC. She is a journalist in Los Angeles.
- **Melina Zuniga** is a graduate of Spelman College and earned a medical degree from the Morehouse School of Medicine. She is a psych/med resident at Tulane University.
- **Lily Larsen** attends Santa Monica College and is a Mid City Neighborhood Council Youth Representative. She founded adolescentactivist.com to inform Los Angeles teens about opportunities for community involvement and civic leadership, and plans to run for L.A. City Council in 2020.
- **Miranda Rector** is an undergraduate student at Yale University. Last summer she studied abroad in Singapore, and she works as a health advocate for Planned Parenthood New England.
- **Pamela Avila** graduated from UC Santa Cruz with a BA in English Language and Literature and spent a semester abroad at Trinity College in Dublin. She is a social media manager at *Los Angeles* magazine.
- **Adre Yusi** graduated from Kalamazoo College with a BA in English with Writing Emphasis and a Media Studies Concentration. She studied in Madrid, Spain, and is a copywriter working in Los Angeles.

MENTORING

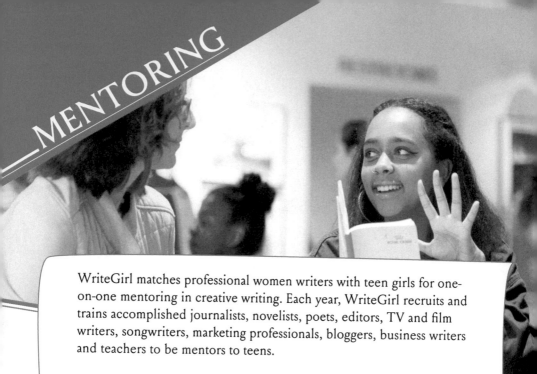

WriteGirl matches professional women writers with teen girls for one-on-one mentoring in creative writing. Each year, WriteGirl recruits and trains accomplished journalists, novelists, poets, editors, TV and film writers, songwriters, marketing professionals, bloggers, business writers and teachers to be mentors to teens.

Every week, mentoring pairs write at coffee shops, libraries, museums and other creative locations. Pairs write, talk and inspire each other to share their stories and invent new worlds. Mentoring relationships last throughout the duration of a girl's participation in the program (often four to five years), and many mentoring bonds continue long after the girl has gone on to college.

WriteGirl continues to expand its In-Schools / Bold Ink Writers Program to offer mentoring and creative writing workshops for incarcerated and systems-impacted boys and co-ed groups, giving them the tools and support they need to complete an educational foundation and set out on a path to personal and professional success.

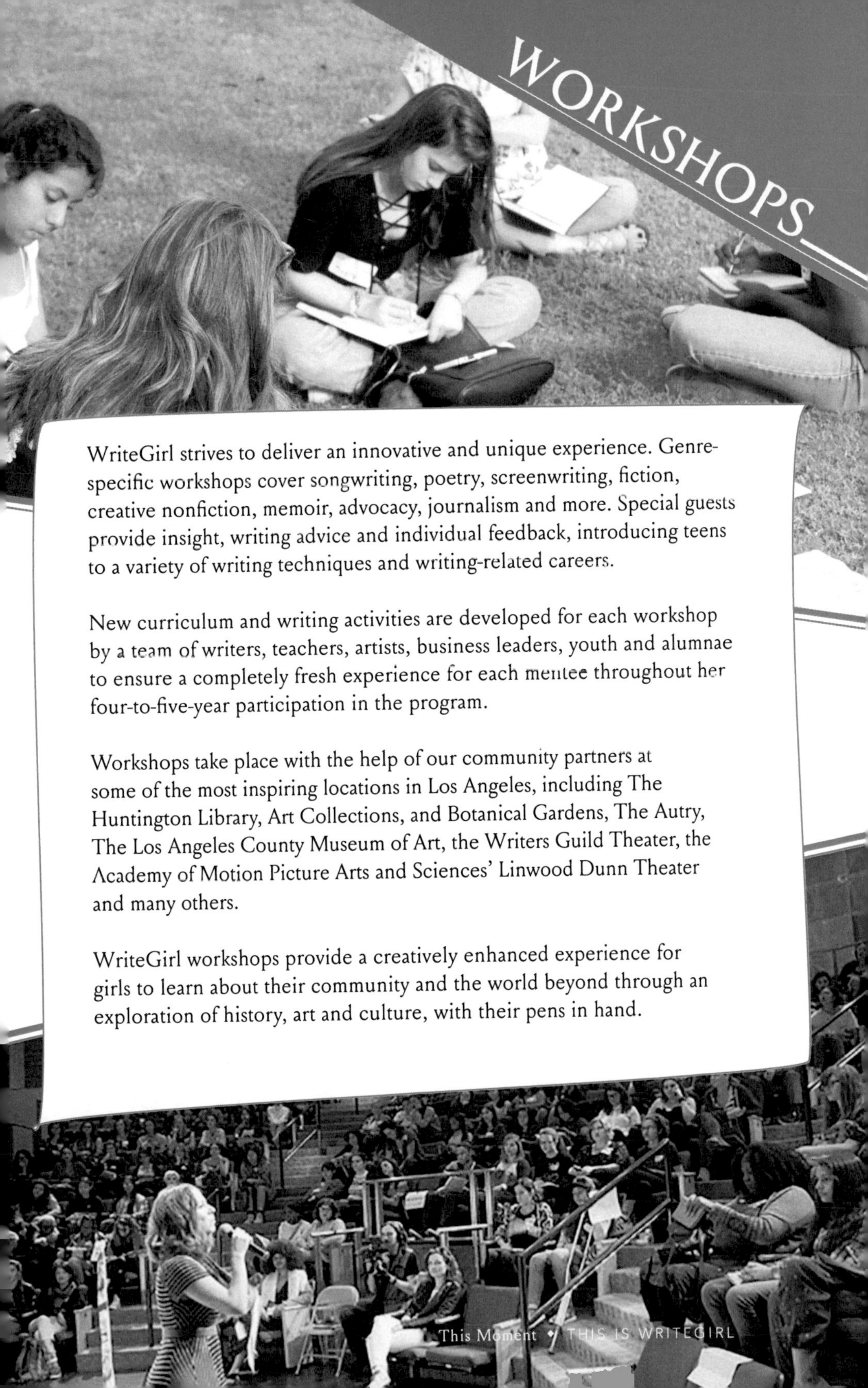

WORKSHOPS

WriteGirl strives to deliver an innovative and unique experience. Genre-specific workshops cover songwriting, poetry, screenwriting, fiction, creative nonfiction, memoir, advocacy, journalism and more. Special guests provide insight, writing advice and individual feedback, introducing teens to a variety of writing techniques and writing-related careers.

New curriculum and writing activities are developed for each workshop by a team of writers, teachers, artists, business leaders, youth and alumnae to ensure a completely fresh experience for each mentee throughout her four-to-five-year participation in the program.

Workshops take place with the help of our community partners at some of the most inspiring locations in Los Angeles, including The Huntington Library, Art Collections, and Botanical Gardens, The Autry, The Los Angeles County Museum of Art, the Writers Guild Theater, the Academy of Motion Picture Arts and Sciences' Linwood Dunn Theater and many others.

WriteGirl workshops provide a creatively enhanced experience for girls to learn about their community and the world beyond through an exploration of history, art and culture, with their pens in hand.

SPECIAL GUESTS

Special guests at WriteGirl (2017 - 2019) include:

College Workshops

Nancy Alderete
Roxana Carrillo
Jamie-Lee Josselyn
Amanda Pendolino

Creative Nonfiction and Memoir

Rory Green
Alex McCale

Fiction

Jennifer J. Chow
Jessica Cluess
Alexa Donne
Marissa Kennerson
Molly Knox Ostertag
Kim Purcell
Lilliam Rivera
Cynthia D'Aprix Sweeney

Directing

Jane Anderson
Barbara Benedek
Aeysha Carr
Nkechi Okoro Carroll
Lisa Cholodenko
Susanna Fogel
Grainne Godfree
Jessica Goldstein
Catherine Hardwicke
Heather Hach Hearne
Liz Kruger
Josann McGibbon
Lisa McQuillan
Jamie Pachino
Lauren Miller Rogen
Diane Ruggiero
Clare Sera
Rippin Sindher
Susan Streitfeld
Courtney Turk
Kelley Turk
Celeste Vasquez

Journalism

Laura Castañeda
Laura E. Davis
Tamara Duricka Johnson
Katie Geyer
Elaine Low
Priska Neely
Stacy Scholder
Miki Turner
Beverly White

Poetry

Ryka Aoki
Neelanjana Banerjee
Ashaki Jackson
VerLacy Jordan
Rachel Kaminer McLeod
Corinna McClanahan Schroeder
Yazmin Monet Watkins

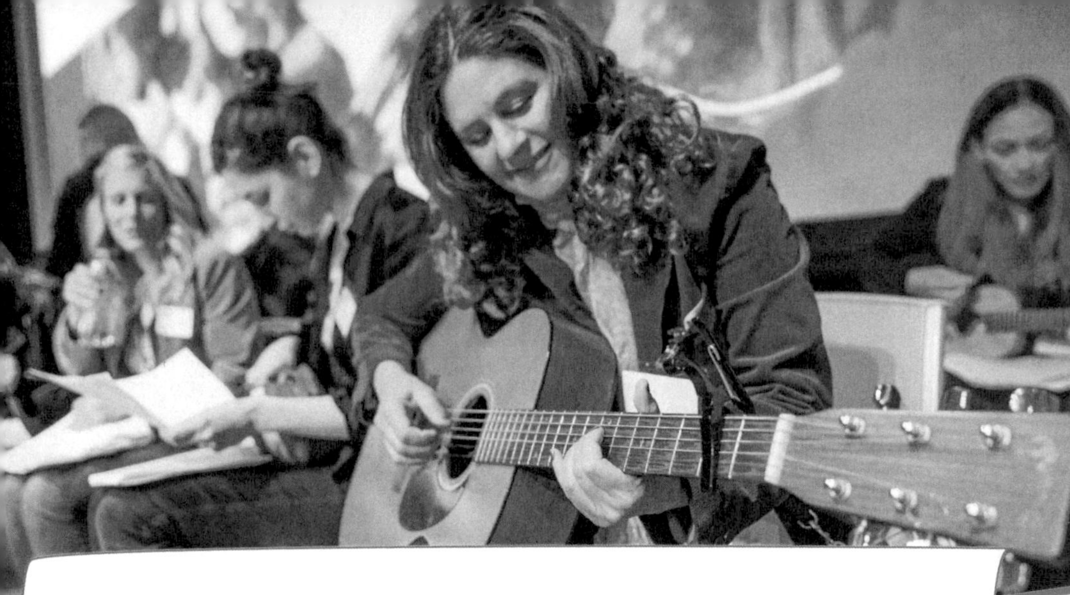

Songwriting

Special thank you to Michelle Lewis for helping create and lead our annual Songwriting Workshop for nearly two decades! You've got the magic touch!

Blush Atterberry
Mai Bloomfield
Jacq Becker
DeAnna Carpenter
Deanna Dellaciopa
Nina Diaz
Miny Duponte
Kyler England
Lauren Evans
Michelle Featherstone
Laurie Geltman
Louise Goffin
Rosi Golan
Kay Hanley
Michelle Lewis
Tova Litvin
Lisa Loeb
Eden Malakouti
Kelly Marie Martin
Clare Means
MILCK
Eve Nelson
Holly Palmer
Shelley Peiken
Anne Preven
Lindy Robbins
Heidi Rojas
Autumn Rowe
Lucy Schwartz
Renee Stahl
Lindsey Stirling
Rosemarie Tan
Keren Taylor
Yahan Yousaf
Yasmin Yousaf

Screenwriting, TV Writing, Playwriting & Performance Workshop Leaders

Lisa Braithwaite
Jessica Hemingway
Clare Sera
Lucé Tomlin-Brenner

Speakers

Lauren Graham
Brandra Ringo
Brandee Stilwell

Actors

Keiko Agena
Cristela Alonzo
Donielle Artese
Alison Becker
Landry Bender
Wayne Brady
Ted Cannon
Ashley Clements
Lauren Donzis
Jessica Garcia
Stephanie Katherine Grant
Kirby Howell-Baptiste
Anne Judson-Yager
Wendi McLendon-Covey
Edi Patterson
Seth Rogen
Robin Weigert
Tom Williamson

WriteGirl teens read their work at public events all over Los Angeles and discover that telling their stories in front of a live audience is fun and empowering.

Each year, WriteGirl produces several readings at a wide variety of civic events and local venues, including Skylight Books, Los Angeles Public Library and the Writers Guild Theater.

WriteGirl is bringing the magic of a WriteGirl workshop to the public with its first-ever WriteGirl webcast, beginning with a Performance Techniques Workshop in 2019. The webcasts allow for girls and women outside of Los Angeles to learn a variety of writing and performance techniques, and get inspired to explore their creative voices.

Thank you to more than 150 schools and dozens of organizations and individuals in the Los Angeles region who promote WriteGirl to teen girls and refer them to WriteGirl. WriteGirl aims to work with girls who need the mentoring support and intercultural exchange that we offer, and we are grateful for all of the teachers, counselors, principals and community leaders who support WriteGirl.

"EVERY TIME A GIRL STANDS UP TO READ, I AM IN AWE OF WHAT SHE SAYS."

– A WRITEGIRL MENTOR

WRITEGIRL IN THE COMMUNITY

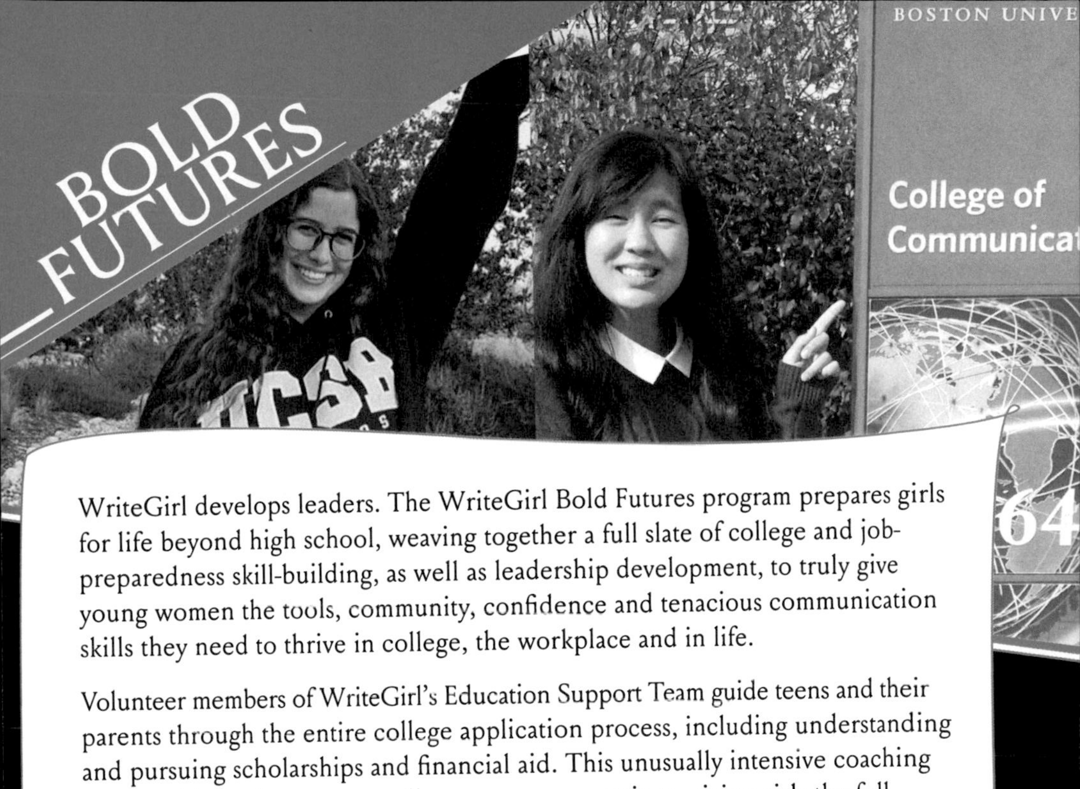

WriteGirl develops leaders. The WriteGirl Bold Futures program prepares girls for life beyond high school, weaving together a full slate of college and job-preparedness skill-building, as well as leadership development, to truly give young women the tools, community, confidence and tenacious communication skills they need to thrive in college, the workplace and in life.

Volunteer members of WriteGirl's Education Support Team guide teens and their parents through the entire college application process, including understanding and pursuing scholarships and financial aid. This unusually intensive coaching is offered in both group as well as one-on-one sessions, giving girls the full support they need to successfully gain access to higher education.

Beyond college, many WriteGirl alumnae are also moving on to advanced studies and professional training, including national and international fellowships such as the Fulbright, and law school, medical school and graduate programs in fields that include creative writing, journalism, international relations, psychology and women's studies.

Bold Futures also offers intensive opportunities for high school seniors and college students. Interns in the WriteGirl office participate in activities designed to build marketable office and communications skills. Interns work alongside WriteGirl staff and volunteers, taking ownership of projects, and receive coaching in accountability, communications, time management, teamwork, goal setting, project planning and implementation, self-care and work/life balance, resume writing and networking.

The WriteGirl chant is "Never underestimate the power of a girl and her pen!" We know that the ability to express oneself can empower a young woman throughout her life.

PUBLICATIONS

Since 2001, WriteGirl Publications has been producing award-winning anthologies that showcase the bold voices and imaginative insights of women and girls. Unique in both design and content, WriteGirl anthologies present a wide range of personal stories, poetry, essays, scenes and lyrics. WriteGirl inspires readers to find their own creative voices through innovative writing experiments and writing tips from both teens and their mentors.

Fifteen anthologies from WriteGirl showcase the work of more than 1,000 women and girls. Selections range from serious to whimsical, personal to political, and heartrending to uplifting. WriteGirl anthologies have collectively won 91 national and international book awards!

Pens on Fire, WriteGirl's educator's guide, offers more than 200 inspiring writing experiments for teens and adults. Through the innovative use of props, movement, art, music, textures, scents and even flavors, Pens on Fire offers step-by-step creative writing curricula for teachers and youth leaders.

ForeWord Reviews, School Library Journal, Kirkus, Los Angeles Times Book Review, The Writer Magazine, Ms. Magazine and *VOYA* have all raved about WriteGirl books.

"Captivating and emotional from the first entry to the last . . ."

– *School Library Journal* review for *You Are Here*

"For these girls (and their mentors) writing is a lens, a filter, a way to cut through the nonsense and see the possibilities . . . [*Nothing Held Back*] suggests that reports of literacy's death have been greatly exaggerated, that language remains a transformative force . . ."

– David Ulin, *Los Angeles Times Sunday Book Review* for *Nothing Held Back*

Support WriteGirl. Buy Our Anthologies!

ALL PROCEEDS BENEFIT WRITEGIRL PROGRAMS

Order WriteGirl books from WriteGirl.org, Amazon.com or bookstores nationwide.

Lights, Camera, WriteGirl! is the annual WriteGirl red carpet benefit where celebrity actors perform monologues and scenes written by WriteGirl teens at our Character & Dialogue Workshop. The workshop is a thrilling chance for teen girls to write, guided by Hollywood screenwriters and playwrights.

The fundraiser includes a silent auction, reception and red carpet interviews. Acclaimed actors bring the girls' writing to life onstage, and a special guest panel of television writers, screenwriters and playwrights offer commentary.

At the 2019 event, hosted by Lauren Graham (*Gilmore Girls*), scenes and monologues written by the girls were performed by Seth Rogen (*Superbad*), Wayne Brady (*Whose Line Is It Anyway?*), Keiko Agena (*Gilmore Girls*), Wendi McLendon-Covey (*The Goldbergs*), Kirby Howell-Baptiste (*Barry*) and Stephanie Katherine Grant (*The Goldbergs*).

A panel of accomplished women screenwriters provided commentary on the scenes. Screenwriters included Clare Sera (*Smallfoot, Blended*), Josann McGibbon (*Descendants*), Liz Kruger (*Salvation*), Heather Hach Hearne (*Freaky Friday*), Nkechi Okoro Carroll (*Bones*), Lisa Cholodenko (*The Kids Are All Right*) and Lauren Miller Rogen (*Like Father*).

WriteGirl is grateful to the Academy of Motion Picture Arts and Sciences for hosting Lights, Camera, WriteGirl! at the Linwood Dunn Theater in Hollywood.

2019 Lights, Camera, WriteGirl! Host Committee: Clare Sera, Jane Anderson, Barbara Benedek, Allison Deegan, Grainne Godfree, Lauren Graham, Heather Hach Hearne, Jennifer Hoppe, Erica Shelton Kodish, Jenji Kohan, Liz Kruger, Lauren Levine, Josann McGibbon, Lisa McQuillan, Nancy Meyers, Melissa Rosenberg and Robin Swicord.

Thank you to our sponsors: The Academy of Motion Picture Arts and Sciences, ICM Partners, HBO, CAA, Sony Pictures WAVE, Sprinkles, Dream Team Directors, Alligator Pear Catering and Hansen, Jacobson, Teller, Hoberman, Newman, Warren, Richman, Rush and Kaller & Gellman, LLP.

“LOOK OUT, MALE-DOMINATED HOLLYWOOD. GIRL SCREENWRITERS ARE COMING FOR YOUR JOBS!”

– A WRITEGIRL MENTOR

"WRITEGIRL CHANGED MY LIFE. I HAVE GROWN IN MY CONFIDENCE, WRITING ABILITY AND MY PASSION FOR STORYTELLING."

– A WRITEGIRL ALUM

> "I LIKE HOW YOU TRULY HAVE NO LIMITS. YOU HAVE THE ABILITY TO THINK WHAT YOU WANT, WRITE WHAT YOU WANT AND JUST BE WHO YOU WANT."
>
> – A WRITEGIRL TEEN

THE WRITEGIRL "ENGINE"

Executive Director
Keren Taylor

Associate Director
Allison Deegan

Managing Director
Katie Geyer

Curriculum Director
Kirsten Giles

Development Associate
Cindy Collins

College Program Manager
Leslie Awender

Administrative Manager
Megan Bennett

Bold Ink Program Specialist
Hazel Rose

In-Schools Program Associate
Stevie Taylor

Bold Ink Writers Workshop Leaders
Natalie Meadors
Kerry McPherson
Nancy Murphy
Jaquita Ta'le

Book Manager
Annlee Ellingson

Event Assistants
Beka Badila
Andrea Esparza
Alex McCale
Lindsay Mendoza
Sally Mercedes

Tech Support
Sable Cantus

Event Support
Pete Hieatt / Deluxe Plants

Website, Branding, Book Design, Graphics
Sara Apelkvist, Isabelle Carasso, Nathalie Gallmeier, Juliana Sankaran-Felix

Photography/Videography
Sarah Anderson, Bayou Bennett, Patrick Burton, Stacy Conner, Saliha Crespo, Vanessa Crocini, Dream Team Directors, Erin Dorothy Photos, Luke Grigg at Circle3Productions, Thomas Hargis, Katherine Leon, Morgan Lieberman, Daniel Lir, Mitch Maher, Daniela Mayock, Molly Stinchfield Photography, Nicole Ortega, Morgan Pirkle, Jackie Rodman, Sarah Rosemann, Miranda Suess, Sophie Webb

" I LOVE THE SISTERHOOD, NO MATTER OUR BACKGROUNDS. "
– A WRITEGIRL TEEN

College Interns

Sofia Aguilar
Melina Almanza
Jessica Bray
Jamie Chen
Marla Cueva
Charlie Dodge
Reina Esparza
Dory Graham
Joy Gursky
Kasey Han
Taya Kendall
Anna Lee
Kai McDaniel
Isabeau Noga
Ana Ortiz
Khamil Riley
Sequoia Sherriff
Tiffany Shin
Catherine Shonack
Deborah Shonack
Madeline Taylor
Jacqueline Uy
Shakyra Walker
Adre Yusi

Special thanks to the Los Angeles County Arts Commission for providing a special summer internship placement for a college student at WriteGirl.

Fellows

Ericka Anderson
Morgan Radford

High School Interns

Pepper Campbell
Sneh Chachra
Lauren Cook
Aleea Evangelista
Sabina Garcia
Addissyn House
Savannah House
Kennedy McIntosh
Sandra Moore
Sofía Salazar
Mya Reyes-Rios
Mercedes Solaberrieta
Elizabeth Surman

"I WAS TOLD TO WRITE FROM MY HEART BECAUSE NO ONE ELSE SEES THE WORLD LIKE I DO."

We are grateful for inspiring event locations for our creative writing workshops and special events: The Academy of Motion Picture Arts and Sciences, The Armory Center for the Arts, The Autry Museum of the American West, The Geffen Contemporary at MOCA, GenHERation Discovery Days, Glendale Downtown Central Library, The GRAMMY Recording Academy, The Huntington Library, Art Collections, and Botanical Gardens, The Japanese American National Museum, LA84 Foundation, Los Angeles County Museum of Art, The National Center for the Preservation of Democracy, The Secret Society of the Sisterhood, USC Annenberg School for Communication and Journalism, Warner Bros., Whitmore Rare Books and the Writers Guild Theater.

Special thanks to The Huntington Library, Art Collections, and Botanical Gardens for their generous support of workshops and events. Our girls and volunteers gain tremendous inspiration from the art, gardens, staff and special events. The Huntington is an oasis in the city, and we are grateful to bring our members to write in this unique environment.

Our girls, volunteers and alumnae have benefited greatly from special events and opportunities in the community. Thank you to ABC7, Amazon Studios, Association of Writers & Writing Programs Conference & Bookfair, Elizabeta Betinski and bardoLA, City of Los Angeles Department of Cultural Affairs, Exposition Review, Renée Fox, Fox Gives, Louise Goffin, Catherine Hardwicke and Sony Pictures, Inner Voice Artists and YouthMundus, Invest in Youth Coalition, Kung Fu Monkey Productions, L.A. Youth Creativity Summit, Michelle Lewis, Los Angeles County Arts Commission, Mattel, Meltdown Comics, Neptunian Woman's Club, Obama Foundation, Pasadena Festival of Women Authors, Pollen Pictures, Kim Purcell, Russia Mentor Network, Sony Pictures WAVE, Soroptimist International of Glendale, State Farm Neighborhood Sessions with iHeartRadio featuring Lindsey Stirling, TEDxPasadena, Tupperware Party Improv, Urban Word's Los Angeles Youth Poet Laureate program, Warner Bros., Women of Warner and Women's March Los Angeles.

In August 2018, **the Obama Foundation's Community Leadership Corps** invited WriteGirl / Bold Ink Writers to work with 300 teens and young adults in Phoenix, Chicago and Columbia, S.C. WriteGirl staff and two alumnae helped corps members prepare and present community action plans and proposals to benefit their home communities. WriteGirl hosted a musical showcase at the end of each three-day event, featuring local musicians and songs written by WriteGirl team members using words and phrases from program participants. WriteGirl also participated in the 2018 Obama Foundation Summit in Chicago, helping coach program finalists to persist in their projects.

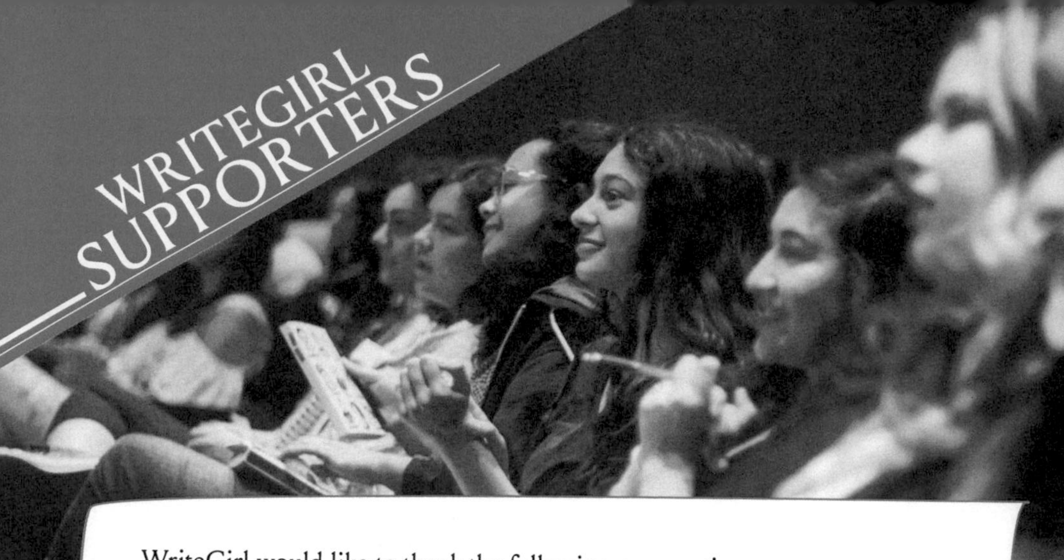

WriteGirl would like to thank the following corporations, government agencies, foundations and individuals for their substantial and generous support:

Barbara Abercrombie

Adams Family Foundation

Stephanie Allen

Amazon Literary Partnership

Jane Anderson and Tess Ayers

Annenberg Foundation

Art for Justice Fund / Rockefeller Philanthropy Advisors

Arts for Incarcerated Youth Network

ASCAP Foundation Irving Caesar Fund

Catherine Auman

Walter Bagley

ban.do

BanterGirl LLC

Aimee Bender

Barbara Benedek

Shelley Berger

Hanna Bowman

Maisha Brown

BranDee Bruce

Anna Bulbrook

Ashley Bush

David Butze

BuzzFeed OYB

California Community Foundation

The Capital Group Companies Charitable Foundation

The Carl & Roberta Deutsch Foundation / HALO Award

Kelly Caves

Kelly Chambers

Jade Chang

Angela Chavez

Chromatic Inc.

City of Los Angeles Department of Cultural Affairs

Tegan Cohan

CohnReznick

Community Works Youth Development

The Coopersmith Family Foundation

Brian Cox

Elizabeth Craft

Crail-Johnson Foundation

Creative Artists Agency

Stephanie Culver

Lynne Danco

Danielle LaPorte Inc.

Allison Deegan

Amy Demas

Susan Dickes

Disney Ears to You

DriveWise Auto

Dwight Stuart Youth Fund

Ebell Rest Cottage Association

Edythe Miller Family Trust

Fielding Edlow

Edlow Family Fund

Elizabeth George Foundation

Annlee Ellingson

Janis Finkle

Frieda C. Fox Family Foundation

Jill Friesen

Frog Crossing Foundation

FX Networks

Sera Gamble

Kathryn Gamel

Diane and Harry Gerst

Terry Gilman, Mysterious Galaxy Bookstore

Grainne Godfree

Jessica Goldstein

GoodAdviseHers

Good Works Foundation

Lauren Graham

Gramercy Group

Stephanie Katherine Grant

Rory Green

Lorvben Grell

Pamela Guest

Capri Haga

Elizabeth Hailey

Hansen, Jacobson, Teller, Hoberman, Newman, Warren, Richman, Rush, Kaller & Gellman, LLP

Jonathan Hanwit

Catherine Hardwicke

HBO

Heather Hach Hearne

Herb Alpert Foundation

Marc Hernandez

David Hochman

The Human Family Educational and Cultural Institute/HUMANITAS

Alison Hills

Sherre Hirsch

Winnie Holzman and Paul Dooley

Jennifer Hoppe

Adele House

Omega Hsu

ICM Partners

Jackie Collins Estate

Melissa Johnson

Peggy Johnson

Joseph H. and Florence A. Roblee Foundation

Ksenia Jury

Barbara Katz

Deana Katz

Kathryn Kay

Lauren Kay

Karey Kirkpatrick

Howard Klein, HBK Investments

Erica Kodish

Jenji Kohan

Kroger

Rachel Kropa

Elizabeth Kruger

Mary Lang

Danielle Lefer

Jonathan Lennox, Mopo Management

Tiffany Lerman

Lauren Levine

Melanie Lewis

LifeLab LLC

Attica Locke

Leslie Locken

Susan London

Los Angeles County Arts Commission

Los Angeles County Office of Education

Los Angeles County Probation Department

Los Angeles Unified School District

Gusti Lowenberg

LSC Communications

Kaila Luna

Christina Lynch

Diane Manuel

Marlborough School / Violets' Giving Circle

John Marshall

Nandita Patel Marshall

Emily Mast

Mattel Children's Foundation

Max H. Gluck Foundation

John McCabe

Carol Meadors

Barbara McCole

McCue Marketing Communications

Tyler McFadden

Angela McFarlin

Josann McGibbon

Lisa McQuillan

Miranda Mengis

Nancy Meyers

Lynne Miller

Thomas Miller

Jay Moriarty

M.S. Grumbacher Foundation

Nancy Murphy

Tina Myers

Mystery Writers of America

Robin Nahin

Susan Bay Nimoy

Karen Noga

Nordstrom

Crosby Noricks, PR Couture

Obama Foundation

Sandra O'Briant

Oder Family Foundation

Maria Ortega

Jessica Parker

Pasadena Literary Alliance

Sonali Patel

Edi Patterson

Cindy Peyton

Phi Beta Kappa Society

Hudson Phillips

Joy & Gerald Picus

Desiree Portillo-Rabinov

Shantel Powell

Kim Purcell

Bonne Radford

The Ralph M. Parsons Foundation

Random Tuesday Inc. / Chilton Running Club

Red Hearts Club of Santa Clarita Valley

Lisa Richwine

Josh Riedford

Riverstreet Productions

Lindy Robbins

Stefani Robinson

Lauren Miller Rogen and Seth Rogen

Melissa Rosenberg and Lev L. Spiro

Ari Rutenberg

Sacred Fools Theater Company

Samuel Eells Literary and Educational Foundation

Elizabeth Sayre

Will Sera

Skylight Foundation

Karin Slaughter Family Charitable Fund

DaVida Smith

Gerrie Smith

Keri Smith

Ashley Elizabeth Solorzano

Songwriters of North America

Sony Pictures Entertainment WAVE

Sony / ATV Music Publishing

Soroptimist International of Glendale

Kathy Spanberger

Lorna St. John

Renee Stahl

Stand Up To Cancer / Entertainment Industry Foundation

Catherine Standiford

Marc and Eva Stern Foundation

Swedish Giant Productions / Wendi McLendon-Covey

Cynthia Sweeney

Robin Swicord

Keren Taylor

Judith Teitelman

Camille Tennyson

Alex Tievy

Robert Tourtellotte

Corinne Tripp

21st Century Fox America Inc. / Fox Gives

Twentieth Century Fox Film Foundation

Marie Unini

Pam Veasy

Linda Venis

Margaret Verrone

VOS Financial

Warner Bros. Impact / DC Entertainment

Warner Bros. / Women of Warner

Dana Watson

Meg Webb

Weingart Foundation

Matty Wilder

Dorothy Winslow

Edward Winterer

Stefanie Jane Woodburn

Rebecca Wurzer

Yes To Inc.

Cathleen Young

Vivian Zaks

Sydney Zhang

WRITEGIRL
WOULD LIKE TO THANK

All of our individual donors who have so generously contributed to help WriteGirl grow and help more teen girls each year.

All of WriteGirl's mentors and volunteers for mentoring teen girls as well as contributing professional services, including strategic planning, public relations, event coordination, mentoring management, training and curriculum development, catering, financial management and administrative assistance.

The growing WriteGirl alumnae network for volunteering, speaking at events and continuing to inspire our young members.

Board Members for their support and guidance on strategy, fundraising, communications and development of community partnerships.

Civic Leaders: The Honorable Mayor Eric Garcetti, Los Angeles County District Attorney Jackie Lacey, Los Angeles County Supervisor Hilda L. Solis, California State Senator Holly J. Mitchell and Los Angeles City Councilmember Marqueece Harris-Dawson for their support and acknowledgement of WriteGirl's contributions to the community.

Sara Apelkvist for design and branding strategy, including development of WriteGirl's logo, website, press kit, stationery, book design, promotional materials and ongoing support.

Writing Journals:
Amazon Studios, Baron Fig, Brush Dance, Cardtorial, Crane & Co., Compendium Inc., Field Notes, Girl of All Work, Hammerpress, International Arrivals, Knock Knock, Leuchtturm1917, May Designs, Public Supply, Rag & Bone, Rhodia, Rifle Paper Co., Snowfall Productions, Studio C

Gift Books for our Members:
Adaptive Studios, *The Busy Woman's Guide to Writing a World-Changing Book* by Cynthia Morris, *Dawn of Spies* by Andrew Lane, *The Female Lead* by Edwina Dunn, Inner Flower Child Books, *Inspired* by Susan Schaefer Bernardo, *Tarot* by Marissa Kennerson

Food, Snacks and Beverages at WriteGirl Workshops and Special Events:
18 Rabbits, 85°C Bakery Cafe, Alcove Cafe & Bakery, Arcade Coffee Roasters, Bai, Baby Bea's Bakeshop, Bagel Broker, Big Sugar Bakeshop, BoBo's, Border Grill, Boxed Water, Cafe Dulce, Cake Girl, Califia Farms, Cocomels, Cucina & Amore, DeLuscious Cookies & Milk, Drink Simple, Equal Exchange, Good Heart Catering, Heath & Lejeune, Hint Water, Hippeas, Kettle Glazed Doughnuts, KIND, Lagunitas Brewing Company, Lucky Boy, Madkins Catering, McCue Communications, Milk Jar Cookies, Nairn's, Natierra, Nothing Bundt Cakes, Oatmega, Purgatory Pizza, Rhythm Superfoods, Saffron Road, Shakey's Pizza, Spindrift, Spitz, Stash Tea, Stella Barra Pizzeria, St. Felix Hollywood, Three Weavers Brewing Company, True Food Kitchen, Uncle Paulie's Deli, Vegan Rob's, Verve Coffee Roasters, Vinovore, VOCO, Waiakea, Weird Wave Coffee Brewers

Alligator Pear Catering and Sprinkles for delectable food for our annual Lights, Camera, WriteGirl! benefit.

Panda Cares/Panda Express for their longtime support of our annual Character & Dialogue Workshop by providing volunteers and delicious food for our members.

Sharky's Woodfired Mexican Grill for amazing food for our annual Season-End Celebration.

Gifts for Girls, Members & Special Events:
Algenist, Ample Hills Creamery, Ariel Cannon Photography, ban.do, *Big Mouth* (Netflix), Blue Q, Credo Beauty, The Duchess Yacht Charter Service, Esqueleto, FACE Stockholm, Fourth & Heart, Greenbar Distillery, Hurraw! Balm, Kikkerland, Nick Kroll, LA Opera, Kimpton La Peer Hotel, *Late Night with Conan O'Brien*, Los Angeles Film Critics Association, Lululemon, Lush, Mad Hippie, NYX Professional Makeup, OOLY, Phyto USA, Playtone/Tom Hanks, Ping Identity, Poketa, PopSockets, Puracy, Roclord Studio, Sakura Color Products of America, SmartyPants Vitamins, Soko Glam, Solmate Socks, Taupe Coat, Toca Madera, UCLA Extension, Warner Bros., Whitmore Rare Books, Yes To, Yogi Tea, Youth To The People

Printing and Copy Services: Chromatic Inc. Lithographers, FedEx Office, LSC Communications

Special thanks to the dozens of generous companies and individuals who donated items for our silent auctions and raffles!

A

Ababon, Makena 94
Agbede, Dana 275
Aghajanian, Zenopia 157
Aguilar, Yvette 261
Alarcio, Rachel 278
Alm-Clark, Faith 119
Alvarez, Jacqueline 76
Arjoon, Kendall 207
Armijo, Allison 256
Arutunian, Anna 183

B

Balbuena, Diana 124
Baranets, Anya 184
Becaria, Samantha 45
Billings, Kumari 255
Blueford, Sydnee 271
Bogen-Froese, Blossom 206
Bradley, Sky 204
Brainin, Xela 199
Braman, Dava 292
Brennan, Cassie 168
Brewster, Eva 86
Brown, Cashmeir 186
Brumer, Delilah 298
Bruno, Brielle 263
Bryce, Devon 91

C

Cage, Kimari 259
Calderon, Olivia 80
Campbell, Samantha 188
Carter, Sarah 48
Ceerla, Clara 210
Chamberlin, Ava 290
Chamberlin, Gillian 77
Chavez, Valerie 107
Cheung, Miranda 244
Chung, Katie 309
Cioni, Makena 203
Cook, Lauren 245
Cortez, Ariana 97
Cox, Akilah 191
Crocker, Brooke 125

D

Davis, Arielle 172
Davis, Cira 205
del Castillo, Danielle 282
Delgadillo, Shirley 284
Dickson, Pearl 57
Dodge, Charlie 226
Donovan, Clare Margaret 174

E

Eller, Lucy 100
Esperon, Kaitlyn 196
Etame, Hyla 238
Evangelista, Aleea 26

F

Fong, Elissa 219
Fong, Juliana Nicole 276
Frohna, Zoe 30, 59, 161
Fung, Lucy 272
Furbert, Alexia 260

G

Garcia, Gianna 72
Garcia, Luna 213
Garcia, Sabina 78
Gerst, Zoe 234
Giammatteo, Culzean 43, 69
Gonzalez, Belen 268
Graham, Helen 37
Graham, Lauren 20
Griffin, Sylvia 215
Guevara, Gabriela 306
Guinnip, Maria 74

H

Han, Jane 89
Harmon, Meagan 133
Harper, Jessica 220
Hayforth, Courtney 243
He, Cynthia 294
Hernandez, Marcela 289
Hirsch, Eden 110
Ho, Alyssa 51, 214, 223
Holland, Serena 270
House, Addissyn 84, 200
House, Savannah 56
Huggins, Madison 25

J

Jeans, Zoe 120
Jean-Sprecher, Ella 310
Jean-Sprecher, Zoe 90
Jefferson, Nicole 36
Johnson, Nia 129
Josephy, Daniella 122, 161
Joya, Jazzmin 66

K

Kandarkar, Ritika 62
Kawsar, Israa 130, 159
Kawsar, Yousra 221
Kendall, Taya 52
Kim, Emma 136
Krug, Samantha 121
Kwon, Macy 112

L

Larsen, Lily 216
Lee, Mina 264
Lewis, Kate 55
Liu, Cindy 131
Lyde, Grace 182

M

Maaloul, Hanna 248
Macias, Liberty 85
Mancera, Denielle 232
Mapa, Indigo 236
Marroquin, Marilyn 103
Martin, Autumn 257
Mashamba, Bibiana 93
Mashamba, Tindi 99
Mason, Lesly 144
McLain, Machaela 302
McLeod, Kaeli 192
Mead, Lily 116
Meah, Faiza 67
Medina, Alejandra 164
Mehta, Kisha 274
Meintjes, Jamie-Lee 138
Mendez, Natalie 44
Mendoza, Brandy 50
Min, Annie 251
Minnis, Georgia 291
Miranda, Heidy Gisselle 195
Mirijanian, Chloë 73, 299
Moore, Sophia 58

O

Orozco, Marina 181

P

Perez, Shani 301
Perkins, Phoebe 96
Petty, Isabel 137
Philadelphia-Kossak, Zoe 126
Pincus, Juliana 224
Pincus, Maya 304
Pineda, Natalie 194
Prado, Joelly 246
Pranger, Alexandra 286
Purcell, Madeline 303

R

Ramirez, Sidny 212
Reiher, Annabel 267
Reyes, Ana 249
Richardson, Sophia 269
Ries, Cora 60
Rincon, Cristal 88
Robles, Melanie 185
Roche, Allyson 83, 239
Roche, Ashley 240
Rodriguez, Alejandra 28
Rogers, Colette 113
Root, Lena 190
Rosales, Victoria 308
Rosenblum, Sophie 27, 71
Rutt, Sophia 34

S

Saadi-Klein, Hana 115
Salamanca, Galylea 231
Salazar, Sofía 114
Saldana, Scarlett 237
Sanchez, Isabella 307
Schlank, Kiyanti 32
Schweiger, Miriam 134
Sekiguchi, Marie 98
Shao, Charlotte 252
Sherriff, Sequoia 106
Shin, Tiffany 161
Shinozaki, Drew 149
Shonack, Catherine 250
Shonack, Deborah 233
Silvia, Sofia 132
Sobrepera, Isabel 288
Solaberrieta, Mercedes 281
Son, Annie 47
Straw, Amber 198
Swanson, Mia 105

T

Taylor, Keren 22
Teachout, Kianna 258
Teraoka, Kendra 178
Thielen, Lauren 38
Thompson, Emmett 40
Toomes, Nyah 163
Tuckness-Kuntz, Emily 46

V

Veloz, Kayla 39
Vigil, Chloë 102
Vincent, Rhema 68

W

Ware, Ashley 222
Washington, Alana 81
Watson, Amayah 166

Y

Youn, Sabrina 262

Z

Zeng, Joanna 277

> "THANK YOU FOR ALL OF THE HARD WORK YOU PUT INTO THESE YOUNG GIRLS. I HAVE WATCHED MY DAUGHTER BLOSSOM INTO A MATURE, RESPONSIBLE, SMART AND INDEPENDENT YOUNG LADY. YOU SHOWED MY DAUGHTER THE WAY. FOR THAT, I WILL FOREVER BE GRATEFUL."
>
> – A WRITEGIRL PARENT

ABOUT THE EDITORS

Keren Taylor, WriteGirl Executive Director, has been a community leader for two decades. In 2001, she founded WriteGirl with the idea of leveraging the skills of women writers to inspire teen girls. Keren has overseen WriteGirl's expansion into a thriving community of women and teen writers and an organization that helps hundreds of Los Angeles girls annually. In November 2013, WriteGirl was honored by First Lady Michelle Obama with the National Arts and Humanities Youth Program Award, the highest national honor awarded to exemplary after-school and out-of-school-time programs from across the country. Keren served as a Community Champion and facilitator for the Annenberg Foundation's Alchemy Program, helping guide nonprofit leaders to organizational success. In 2014, Keren was selected as a CNN Hero, recognizing her efforts to leverage the professional skills of women writers to help youth. In 2018, Keren was invited to serve as a member of the Barbie Global Advisory Council to help shape Mattel Inc.'s "Evolution of Barbie." Keren serves on the board of the Arts for Incarcerated Youth Network (AIYN) and leads WriteGirl's work with incarcerated and systems-impacted teens as a founding member organization of AIYN. Working with a team of editors and designers, Keren has directed the production of more than two dozen anthologies of writing by teen girls and their mentors. To date, WriteGirl publications have been awarded 91 national and international book awards. Passionate about helping women and girls, Keren is a frequent speaker at conferences and book festivals nationwide. Keren is an assemblage artist and mosaicist. She holds a Bachelor's Degree in International Relations from the University of British Columbia, a Piano Performance Degree from the Royal Conservatory of Music, Toronto, and a Diploma from the American Music and Dramatic Academy, New York City.

Allison Deegan, EdD, is a screenwriter who serves as WriteGirl's Associate Director and as a member of the Advisory Board. In addition, she has served as an Associate Editor on all of WriteGirl's award-winning anthologies. She has extensive expertise in supporting incoming and current college and graduate school students, managing youth and writing programs, and supporting creativity and public policy. She is a fiscal and policy administrator with the Los Angeles County Office of Education and an adjunct professor in graduate programs at Cal State Long Beach and Trident University, as well as a private admissions consultant. She holds a BS from Syracuse University, an MFA from the Institute of American Indian Arts, an MPA in Public Policy from California State University, Long Beach, and an EdD in Educational Leadership, also from CSULB.

CONNECT WITH WRITEGIRL

Follow us on **LinkedIn**: linkedin.com/company/WriteGirl

Follow us on **Pinterest**: pinterest.com/WriteGirlLA

Follow us on **Twitter**: twitter.com/WriteGirlLA

Subscribe to our channel on **YouTube**: youtube.com/WriteGirlChannel

Visit our **website**: writegirl.org

Check out our **blog**: writegirl.org/blog

Like us on **Facebook**: facebook.com/WriteGirlOrganization

Follow us on **Goodreads**: goodreads.com/WriteGirlLA

Follow us on **Instagram**: instagram.com/WriteGirlLA

Never underestimate the power of a girl and her pen.

Always be bold and believe in yourself.